SPANISH VERBS
SER and *ESTAR*

Key to Mastering
the Language

by
J. SERRANO and S. SERRANO

HIPPOCRENE BOOKS
New York

For information, address the publisher:
    The Hippocrene Books, Inc.
    171 Madison Avenue
    New York, N.Y. 10016

ISBN 0-7818-0024-2

Second printing, 1996.

First Edition
Printed in the United States of America

TABLE OF CONTENTS

Demystifying Ser and Estar

The purpose of this book is to dispel the aura of mysterious complexity which surrounds *ser* and *estar*. It will show you how to get to grips with the far-reaching and seemingly insurmountable problems caused by these key Spanish verbs. Verbs which are a microcosm of the Spanish language—of how the world is conceptualized in Spanish. They are revelatory of how the Spanish mind works, but they are also a minefield for those who are ignorant of their ramifications. Unless you are aware of this fact, the language barrier will never be breached—no matter how many fancy, colloquial or scholarly expressions are learnt.

In order to use language effectively we have to be able to use it creatively—by employing its structures as the building blocks with which our ideas are constructed. Unless you have a sound grasp of *ser* and *estar* (the two most fundamental building blocks of the Spanish language) your construction will always be faulty.

The difference between these two troublesome little verbs is one of the greatest (and up to now, almost impenetrable) barriers to learning Spanish. They also happen to be among the first structures that learners encounter when commencing their study of the language. Structures which thereafter turn into obstacles blocking the path of all who want to communicate successfully in Spanish. This book will help you break through the barriers which impede progress. It sets out what we believe is a completely new way of understanding these verbs and reveals the fundamental principle which underlies the difference between them. Furthermore, the strategies and explanations contained herein bring this principle within the reach of all learners. You do not have to be a gifted linguist or brainy academic to be able to use these verbs correctly.

All too frequently grammar books and teachers set out rules on when to use one or other of these verbs and then provide a list of 'exceptions' to such rules, or teach (misleadingly) that these verbs are all to do with permanence and transitoriness, or that they are often completely interchangeable. However, the beginner might want to know **WHY**, in Spanish, we say *soy* estudiante (which means I am a student) and not *estoy estudiante*. The learner at the intermediate level might wonder, for example, if it is really the same to say : *No me gusta Juan porque está gordo* and *No me gusta Juan porque es gordo* (I don't like Juan because he is fat). While the advanced level student might ask if the statement 'María is always affectionate' can be translated as: *María siempre está cariñosa* and *María siempre es cariñosa;* or whether the phrases *Juan está soltero* and *Juan es soltero* (which informs us that Juan is not married) carry exactly the same meaning and emphasis, and hence are truly interchangeable.

In fact students of all levels—from beginners to the most advanced—not only have a right to know, but in the case of *ser* and *estar* actually need to know why one or other of these verbs is employed. Such things are rarely 'explained' in grammars and text books, sometimes they are merely stated, or worse, stated inaccurately.

Yet the difference between *ser* and *estar* is a particular instance of how it is only when the non-native Spanish speaker really understands the underlying meaning of these structures that he/she is able to use them correctly and effectively. In the case of *ser* and *estar*, this means that learners must be made aware of the

4

cultural background to these verbs, as well as the far-reaching implications still governing their use, before they can master them. This may sound extremely intellectual and complex, but in fact this is not the case. As you will see in Part I of this book, there is a basic, logical and clear difference in the way these verbs function and this can be explained in fairly simple terms.

Part I offers you new insight on how to master *ser* and *estar* so that, in the future, they will work for you instead of against you. You will at last understand how these verbs function and learn to manipulate them skilfully and humorously, as they become the cornerstone of your creative use of the Spanish language. In order to make this first part accessible to all learners, the numerous examples used to illustrate particular points will all be given in the present tense. However, the principles outlined will apply equally to all tenses.

In Part II of the book you will find original material which provides a practical demonstration of the major role *ser* and *estar* play in the art of mastering Spanish: in dialogue; in character sketches; in humorous, insulting and complimentary repartee, etc., as well as their function in more poetic language. These illustrations are of varying degrees of difficulty (from relatively simple to very advanced) and all tenses will be encountered. However, learners will find help in the explanatory notes on vocabulary, idioms, play on words, proverbs, etc.—particularly those relating to *ser* and *estar*—which accompany each text. As a further aid for those who would like a practical demonstration of the use and implications of *ser* and *estar* in these texts, the last chapter is given over to an analysis of the character sketch *Juan el malas pulgas*. It is hoped that this will serve as a guide to the way the other texts should be read and studied.

We believe there is a genuine need for a book which is easy to read and practical, but which does not sacrifice scope or depth in order to achieve its objectives. A book that will be useful to learners throughout the whole of their Spanish language studies—to be dipped into and consulted whenever clarification might be needed. It should prove helpful to all who want to learn to communicate successfully in Spanish: those working on their own, those seeking additional support for class work, those who study Spanish for pleasure, for business, or who want to achieve academic excellence. In fact all who (however great or small their knowledge of Spanish at a particular time) want to use what they already know, or are in the process of learning, more accurately. Learners looking for no more than a survival-kit might find the hints and short-cuts provided here sufficient for their requirements. While those whose needs are greater, should find the book's scope challenging and instructive.

Finally, this book is the product of over twenty years' experience of teaching Spanish at all levels, from absolute beginners to graduate students. Its strategies have been tried and tested over the years. Furthermore, they are strategies which have proved helpful to learners of all ages and levels and we hope they will be just as helpful to you.

PART I

UNDERSTANDING SPANISH THROUGH *SER* AND *ESTAR*

CHAPTER ONE

Ser and *Estar:*
Microcosm of the Spanish Language

I

1. THE ALL-PURPOSE VERB 'TO BE'

Learners of all ages and levels seem to have great difficulty understanding and getting to grips with the different verbs used in Spanish to express what in English comes under the umbrella of the all-purpose verb 'to be'. This is probably not surprising given that:

—   All too often text books and grammar reference books only succeed in either confusing students by creating an aura of mysterious complexity around these verbs, or wearing them down with long lists of rules and exceptions.

—   Many non-native teachers of Spanish have themselves never completely mastered the often subtle differences of meanings conveyed by these verbs—perhaps because as students they too were only given a superficial explanation of this.

—   Many native teachers—who instinctively know how these verbs function—often have difficulty in explaining them to students used to one all-purpose 'to be' verb.

Yet in reality, as you will see, there are **NOT** so many different rules or exceptions. Most of these so-called rules are merely variations of **ONE** main difference in meaning. In English this is often expressed by context, intonation of the voice, etc., while in Spanish different verbs are required to express the different meanings, connotations or nuances conveyed by the all-purpose English verb 'to be'.

Once this basic difference is understood, you will find that Spanish, in this case, is a much more precise language and the accurate application of the Spanish verbs 'to be' serves only to clarify rather than confuse. All those engaged in dialogue will find it is much easier to ascertain the intended meaning, without the constant need of context, intonation or stress: the choice of the relevant Spanish verb is generally sufficient.

In this chapter therefore, we aim to reveal the meaning of these verbs and to focus on the basic principle which underlies the difference in their use.

Once you have digested this principle, you will find that these verbs are not so mysterious and complex as they have been made out to be. You will understand how they function and will realize that this is not the exclusive property of a few gifted and clever linguists, who seem to want to guard their secret jealously. Furthermore, you will be in possession of a very valuable piece of knowledge—a tool which will help you express yourself in Spanish much more accurately, and hence more effectively.

Of course, this does not mean that from now on you will instantly and automatically always use these verbs correctly. Mistakes are bound to be made, especially in the fast exchanges of lively conversation. Do not forget, your mind has been programed over many years to use one all-purpose verb and you will need time to adjust when speaking Spanish. However, you will have a better grasp of how these verbs function, and this will be a major step forward along the road to successful communication in Spanish.

*   *   *

2. TO BE OR NOT TO BE?

In English the verb 'to be' is used indiscriminately to express different concepts. So the first step is to be aware of the various meanings which this verb conveys in English.

If, as an example, we take the simple phrase:

He is so cold*

we obviously understand each word within this phrase but will need a context reference, or some voice intonation, or stress to understand the exact meaning the speaker wishes to convey. The phrase as it stands is ambiguous and would certainly leave any native Spanish speaker confused.

---

* The word 'cold', as 'hot', can have sexual connotations both in English and Spanish, but this we shall deal with later.

'He is so cold' has three obvious possible meanings in English:

> **a)** **He is so cold**—referring to the person's nature, i.e. he is a cold sort of person. It defines his character: he is an undemonstrative person, someone lacking in geniality or affection of others. The verb is identifying an inherent quality or essential characteristic of the person's nature.

> **b)** **He is so cold**—referring only to specific, accidental circumstances. As in, for example, "I don't know what is wrong with John today, he is so cold," meaning he is behaving in a very cold manner, although normally this might not be a label one would use when speaking of John. In fact, John's nature could even be one of geniality, but at the present time, perhaps due to abnormal circumstances, he seems (uncharacteristically) indifferent or distant.

> **c)** **He is so cold**—referring to the way he feels (physically) at the moment, in that, owing to the adverse weather conditions and the very low temperature, he (his body) is feeling very cold.

The equivalent phrase in Spanish, even when taken out of context, would not so easily lend itself to such confusion as, depending on the speaker's intended meaning or emphasis, a different verb would be used to express these three very different concepts.

These concepts, when expressed in Spanish, would correspond to:

a) He is so cold = El *es* tan frío. Here *es* (the 3rd person singular of the verb *ser*) is used to express what is a defining characteristic. It refers to the person's identity or nature. It tells us **WHAT** he is like. So that in this case we are left in no doubt that by nature he is a very cold **sort of** person.

b) He is so cold = El *está* tan frío. Here *está* (the 3rd person singular of the verb *estar*) indicates a state of being at a particular time. It does not refer to the natural, inherent, qualities which make up the person's character. It tells us **HOW** he is—in what state of being he finds himself under certain circumstances, **HOW** he is looking, acting, etc. In the case of John, it indicates **HOW** he is behaving today, and that is in a very cold manner.

c) He is so cold = El *tiene* tanto frío. Here *tiene* (the 3rd person singular of the verb *tener* which means 'to have') is used. Literally this would translate 'He has so much coldness'—that is to say, 'He *has*' in the sense that 'He (his body) *feels* very cold'.

This book is concerned only with the two main meanings of the verb 'to be', that is, the Spanish verbs *ser* and *estar*. The third meaning, *tener*, mentioned above in c), as well as *hacer* (which means 'to do or to make') are not so problematic as they are employed in specific cases. *Hacer*, for instance, is used in Spanish with the weather, in expressions such as *hace frío hoy* ('It is cold today').

15

NOTE:

As mentioned in the Introduction, for pedagogical reasons the examples given to illustrate particular points will only employ the present tense of the verbs *ser* and *estar*. But of course the principle outlined here will apply to all tenses of these verbs.

PRESENT TENSE OF *SER* AND *ESTAR*

	SER	*ESTAR*	TO	BE
yo	*soy*	*estoy*	I	am
tú	*eres*	*estás*	you[1]	are
usted			you[2]	are
él	*es*	*está*	he	is
ella			she	is
nosotros/as	*somos*	*estamos*	we	are
vosotros/as	*sois*	*estáis*	you[3]	are
ustedes	*son*	*están*	you[4]	are
ellos/as			they	are

---

(1) 'You' singular familiar form
(2) 'You' singular polite/formal form
(3) 'You' plural familiar form
(4) 'You' plural polite/formal form

16

3. *SER* or *ESTAR?*

Many text books and teachers still explain the difference in the use of *ser* and *estar* by insisting inaccurately that:

—   *ser* signifies permanence, and denotes a permanent characteristic of the person or thing concerned;

—   *estar* indicates a transitory condition or state.

This explanation of permanence or transitoriness is in fact the cause of much later confusion. For this rule cannot always be relied upon and is often misleading.

An example of this confusion can be found in the phrase 'I am a student' (*soy* estudiante), which in Spanish requires the verb *ser.* Not surprisingly, students who are commencing their studies of Spanish immediately ask why? They waste no time in pointing out that they will be students for a few years only and that their studentship is therefore not a permanent condition. This fact has led them to believe (wrongly) that *estar* should be used.

Confusion regarding the use of these two verbs for 'to be' exists to such an extent that even those who profess to be proficient in Spanish are all too often found writing or saying phrases like *Juan es siempre preocupado,* instead of *Juan está siempre preocupado* (Juan is always worried). Obviously the word *'siempre'* (always) has misled them here into thinking that because Juan is always in such a state, this notion of permanence necessitates the use of the verb *ser.* As we shall see later, the phrase is emphasizing the **STATE** Juan is in (albeit permanently), rather than denoting a characteristic which identifies his nature.

Such confusion arises because the basic difference in meaning between these two verbs has not been either fully explained or grasped. This, we hope, will be clarified by the end of the book.

* * *

4. TO BE OR NOT TO BE—IS THAT *THE* QUESTION?

The following two examples will serve to emphasize the fundamental difference between the verbs *ser* and *estar* and will reveal the basic principle governing their use:

> **A) El azúcar *es* dulce**

> **B) El café *está* caliente**

In the case of **A)** *El azúcar es dulce* (Sugar is sweet), the verb used is **ser** because we are dealing with something that is an inherent quality or attribute of sugar. Sweetness is its defining or identifying characteristic. The verb implies that it is sugar's nature to be sweet for, if it were not sweet, it would be anything but sugar. The verb thus denotes an essential characteristic. It tells us **WHAT** sugar is.

In the case of **B)** *El café está caliente* (The coffee is hot), the verb used is **estar** because here we are talking about the state the coffee is in at the moment: a state of hotness. Hotness is a quality, an attribute, which is totally accidental to the coffee—a circumstantial (and in this

18

(and in this case, also transitory) state for, if left, it will very soon become cold. It tells us nothing about the coffee's inherent characteristic or nature. It does not indicate what coffee is, but **HOW** the coffee is (hot or cold) under particular circumstances.

So that, if we borrow Hamlet's famous phrase and ask if 'to be, or not to be hot' is what makes coffee 'to be' coffee, clearly, the answer is that it is not. For hot, or not hot, coffee is still coffee. The question of its hotness or coldness does not affect its nature. Thus, 'to be or not to be hot' is not really **THE** question when it comes to defining or identifying what coffee is.

However, in the case of sugar, "to be, or not to be sweet" is precisely **THE** question, for the nature of sugar is to be sweet—sweetness is of its essence and is what makes sugar 'to be' sugar.

You will now be able to appreciate the way in which the English verb 'to be' is employed indiscriminately to express both:

— inherent qualities and essential characteristics— **WHAT** kind of thing/person something or someone is (as in A);

— accidental qualities and existential states—**HOW** a person or thing is at a particular time (as in B).

And you will now also be aware of the underlying reason for the use in Spanish of two different verbs.

**The fundamental difference between *ser* and *estar*
is the difference between
WHATNESS and HOWNESS**

Ser = WHATNESS

Ser (most of its forms from the Latin *esse*) is the verb which explicitly refers to the concept or idea of **WHATNESS**. It indicates **WHAT** a thing is: as in the question 'What is John?'(*¿Qué es John?*).

Ser denotes the essence, nature or a defining (in the sense of identifying) characteristic of a person or thing—even if this characteristic is only transitory, as in the statement 'John is a student' (*John es estudiante*). John may well only be a student for a few years, but still a defining or identifying characteristic of John's person now is that of being a student—he is not John *the baker*, but John *the student* of law.

In former times people, when referred to, were almost automatically identified with their trade. This can still be seen in towns and villages in Spain, where you will often hear people say: *Es Rafael el carpintero* (It's Rafael, the carpenter), *Es María la cocinera* (It's María the cook), etc. We can also see something of this in the professions, e.g., *La señora Martínez la abogada* (Señora Martinez the lawyer), and *Es el Dr. López*, where the title 'Dr.' becomes a very obvious part of the person's identity and immediately tells us **WHAT** this person is.

Two useful hints on when to use *ser* are:

SER = IDENTITY OR NATURE

When using the verb 'to be' in Spanish, remember:

1. Any question asking "WHAT..?" or any statement answering the question "WHAT..?", always takes *SER*.

WHAT is he/she?	—	*¿Qué es él/ella?*
WHAT is that?	—	*¿Qué es eso?*
She is a doctor	—	*Ella es médica*
It is a pen	—	*Es una pluma.*

2. Any question asking "WHO..?" or any statement answering the question "WHO..?", always takes *SER*.

WHO is the teacher?	—	*¿Quién es el profesor?*
WHO is that?	—	*¿Quién es ése?*
John is the teacher	—	*John es el profesor*
It is a Peter	—	*Es Peter*

You will appreciate that hint No. 2 is not really different from hint No. 1, as the same principle governs both. For, here again, the question which is being asked is one about the identity of the person concerned; when we ask 'who is..?', we are really asking '**WHAT** is the identity of that person'; '**WHAT** is the name of that person', etc.

Estar = HOWNESS

Estar (from the Latin verb *stare*—in English 'to stand') refers to the state of being of a person or thing at a particular time. It does not serve to emphasize or define identity, nor does it refer to any inherent characteristic. The verb denotes not what but **HOW** a person or a thing is, within a specific space and time—even permanently, as in the phrase *Juan está siempre preocupado* (Juan is always worried/in a worried state). It indicates **HOWNESS**—the state of being, not the nature of being. It tells us **HOW** that person or thing feels, behaves, acts, or appears at a given time.

Two hints on when to use *estar* are:

ESTAR = STATE OF BEING

When using the verb 'to be' in Spanish, remember:

1. Any question asking "HOW is someone?" or any statement answering the question "HOW is someone?", always takes *ESTAR*.

¿Cómo está Juan?	— HOW is Juan?
¿Cómo están los niños?	— HOW are the children?
Sonía está bien	— Sonia is fine
Ellos están regular	— They are not too good

2. Any question meaning "HOW is something?" or any statement answering "HOW is something?" must always use *ESTAR*.

¿Cómo está el vino?	— HOW is the wine?[1]
¿Cómo está el café?	— HOW is the coffee?
Está muy bueno	— It is very good[2]
Está caliente	— It is hot.

---

(1) 'How is the wine?' meaning 'is it to your liking/how do you find it? is it in good condition?

(2) *'Está muy bueno'* meaning 'It is very good/it is to my taste.'
We will deal with this in more detail on pp. 45—48.

Estar = WHERENESS

As we pointed out earlier, **estar** is from the Latin verb *stare* meaning 'to stand' and thus can also denote position or location. It situates something or someone in a particular place, either permanently or temporarily. The following two examples using *ser* and *estar* should clarify this for you:

> A) *Madrid **es** la capital de España*
> B) *Madrid **está** en España*

You will see from example B) *Madrid **está** en España* (Madrid is in Spain), that here the verb **estar** is merely locating or placing Madrid in a particular space—the country of Spain. It indicates **WHERE** Madrid is situated. It tells us nothing about what Madrid is—for this information we must go to example A). In example A) *Madrid **es** la capital de España* (Madrid is the capital of Spain), the phrase is identifying Madrid as the capital city of Spain. It tells us **WHAT** Madrid is, and thus *ser* is used.

Estar can indicate position in two ways:

— in a real, literal, sense as in example A) *Madrid **está** en España;*

— in a figurative, metaphorical, sense as in the phrase *Juan **está** en la luna* (which translates into English literally as Juan is on the moon, but which really means something like Juan has his head in the clouds—he is completely out of touch with reality). The emphasis here is on our image of Juan placed in some figurative location.

24

Two hints on this point:

ESTAR = LOCATION OR POSITION

When using the verb 'to be' in Spanish, remember:

1. Literal position/location:

Any question or statement referring to position—WHERE someone or something is (physically situated)—whether the position be temporary or permanent, must always use *ESTAR:*

WHERE is Paul now?   — *¿Dónde está Paul ahora?*

WHERE is Madrid?   — *¿Dónde está Madrid?*

Paul is in England   —   *Paul está en Inglaterra*

Madrid is in Spain   — *Madrid está en España*

2. Figurative position/location:

Any question or statement referring to position—WHERE someone or something is (figuratively situated)—must always use *ESTAR.*

To be in a jam   — ***Estar** en apuros*
To always have one's
   head in the clouds — ***Estar** siempre en la luna*

CHAPTER TWO

What is the Question?

II

1. IT IS A QUESTION OF CHOICE

Some reference and textbooks still inform learners that *ser* and *estar* are often interchangeable when used with certain qualifying adjectives and words indicating marital status, such as: *gordo/a* (fat), *calvo/a* (bald), *cariñoso/a* (affectionate), *casado/a* (married), etc. In fact this is not totally accurate, as the choice of verb used will denote a difference, to a greater or lesser degree.

With most qualifying adjectives, it is a question of choice as to which verb is used—but this choice will always imply a difference in meaning or emphasis. It will depend on what you want to convey, on your perception or intended meaning. At first sight this may sound rather baffling but, in fact, the choice between *ser* and *estar* is a relatively simple one as, once again, it reflects the difference between **WHATNESS** and **HOWNESS.**

This will be made clear in the following examples:

> 1) *Ser* **viejo**   or   *Estar* **viejo?**

> 2) *Ser* **casado**   or   *Estar* **casado?**

> 3) *Ser* **cariñoso**   or   *Estar* **cariñoso?**

We will look first of all at the adjective *viejo/a* (old), one of the more straightforward cases. Once the difference in meaning between the use of *ser* and *estar* with this word is understood, we can then go on to analyse two of the more problematic cases, using *casado/a* (married), and *cariñoso/a* (affectionate) as our examples. Cases which have led many to believe that these words can often be used indiscriminately with either verb.

1) Viejo/a

If, for instance, we take the phrase:

Antonio *está* viejo

here the use of the verb *estar* indicates that we are not necessarily referring to Antonio's real age. In fact our Antonio is only 29 years old. But his physical state is one of such deterioration for a man of his age that he gives us the impression of being much older than he actually is. It could also mean that Antonio's mentality is so old-fashioned and his way of dressing is so out-moded that, all in all, even though he is still young in years, he is old for his age or at least he appears so to us. Thus in the cases where we are referring to a person's mental or physical state (as in the case of Antonio) we are referring to **HOWNESS: HOW** he appears to us, and hence *estar* must be used.

On the other hand, if we now take Pedro, who is in fact 92 years old, we are talking about someone who is truly and undeniably old in years—he is an old man. Here to express this fact of **WHATNESS: WHAT** Pedro truly is, we must use *ser*. Hence we say without reservation that:

Pedro *es* viejo
Pedro is old

However, in Pedro's case, he happens to be a man who takes such good care of himself: dresses smartly, keeps fit, has such a young mentality etc., that his young outlook and well-conserved condition makes him appear much younger than he actually is. Thus of Pedro one can also say that:

aunque *es* viejo, Pedro *está* joven

although he is old, (in years), Pedro is young (for his age)

2) *Casado/a*

The same principle also applies to words indicating marital status: *casado/a* (married), *soltero/a* (single), *divorciado/a* (divorced).

Normally ***estar*** is used with these words, but this is so because what is usually being emphasized is the state—in this case the marital state (status)—of the person concerned, and thus it denotes **HOWNESS**. Nevertheless, *ser* can also be used with these words though this is less common.

The difference in nuance which results from using ***ser*** or ***estar*** with words indicating marital status is often difficult for non-native Spanish speakers to grasp on first acquaintance. Yet, though in English we cannot avail ourselves of two different 'to be' verbs to express this, nevertheless there are expressions which convey the essence of such a difference.

For example, when we are simply referring to a person's marital status, we might just qualify the person concerned by saying that he/she is married (*casado/a*) or single (*soltero/a*) etc. This would equate with the meaning conveyed by the Spanish word ***estar***:

31

Está **casado/a**

Está **soltero/a**

It indicates the marital position. In plain terms, it tells us **HOW** the person is situated, **HOW** he/she stands marriage-wise.

On the other hand, if we want to indicate that the person concerned is a bachelor, a confirmed bachelor, a spinster, an old maid etc., with all the implications these concepts convey, then to express this in Spanish *ser* is used as, for example, in the phrase:

Es **soltero/a**

Here, what is really being said is:

Es [*un hombre/una mujer*] *soltero/a*

Es [*un/una*] *soltero/a*

or

Es [*una persona*] *soltera*

So that when using *ser* in the phrase '*es soltero/a*' we are explicitly defining the person by attaching a label or name to him/her. Thus *soltero/a* becomes a name or noun. And once we find ourselves dealing with a noun, we are automatically in the realm of identifying—literally putting names to people and things so as to identify and define them. We are in the realm of **WHATNESS,** and hence *ser* is required.

Taking the statement *José es soltero,* it will now be clear that this phrase is elliptical—it is a short form for *José es [un hombre] soltero,* or *José es [un] soltero.* And the English equivalent of both these phrases is José is a bachelor. In both Spanish and English the verb 'to be' is here denoting **WHAT** José is, and labels him a bachelor.

It is perhaps the elliptical or shortened nature of the phrases, in cases such as the above, which causes the confusion and difficulty experienced by students when trying to express these ideas in Spanish. They often do not realize that the phrase, for instance, *Julia es divorciada* is a short form of:

Julia es [*una*] divorciada

or

Julia es [*una persona*] divorciada

Julia is a divorcee

And as soon as we say that someone or something is '**a**' something we are automatically defining the person or thing and thus talking about **WHATNESS.** This remains true whether the indefinite article (*un/una*) is explicitly mentioned, as in *Julia es* **una** *divorciada,* or whether it is merely implicit in the elliptical phrase, as in *Julia es divorciada.*

This will perhaps be clearer if we look at the English expressions such as 'He is a confirmed bachelor', 'She is an old maid' or 'He is a happily married man', etc. In such expressions, although the marital status of the person is of course alluded to, the statement is not really emphasizing this. Rather it is referring to the image or concept of **WHAT** it is to be a 'confirmed bachelor' or 'an old maid' etc. It embraces all the many essential characteristics which go towards identifying the idea, concept or nature of such a person—and tells us the sort of person he/she is. Thus it provides us with an identifiable image of **WHAT** this person is.

Taking as an example the phrase 'She is an old maid', the characteristics which this image or concept conjures up might be: fussiness, old-age, someone who is perhaps rather puritanical and set in her way, etc., and of course it also implies that the person is not married. But the emphasis is not just on the last factor (her marital status). It embraces all the other characteristics which go towards giving us the rather pejorative image of what it is to be 'an old maid' and this meaning is conveyed in Spanish by the use of *ser.*

Curiously, although in English there is not such a pejorative image for an unmarried man—'confirmed bachelor' is certainly not as derogatory as 'old maid'—in Spanish the same expression is used for both sexes*.

Ana *es* una solterona* — Ana is an old maid

Pablo *es* un solterón* — Pablo is a confirmed bachelor

* By adding the augmentative suffix or ending *ón/ona* to the word *soltero/a* we get: *solterón* (confirmed bachelor) and *solterona* (spinster or old maid—depending on context).

Many grammar books set out the so-called rule that, with words indicating marital status, *ser* is normally used when addressing strangers, e.g.:

¿*Es usted casado?*

while friends renewing acquaintance would use *estar*, asking:

¿*Estás casado?*

However, this 'rule' is not a result of the arbitrariness of language, as has often been implied. In fact, it is a logical application of the **WHATNESS** and **HOWNESS** principle. Clearly, two strangers would usually be asking for information regarding each other's identity, and thus use **ser**. Whereas old friends meeting again would not need to approach the question from the point of view of identity. They would simply be enquiring if there had been any change in each other's (marital) circumstances since they last met, and hence would employ **estar**.

3) *Cariñoso/a*

We will now move on to the case of *cariñoso/a* (affectionate) and, more specifically, when used with the word *siempre* (always). The addition of *siempre* here seems to narrow the gap between the two verbs and therefore helps to make the distinction less obvious.

Taking the following two phrases:

María siempre *está* cariñosa.
María siempre *es* cariñosa.

it is often suggested that these expressions are interchangeable. However if by 'interchangeable' it is meant that they have exactly the same meaning and emphasis, this is not really true. Just as in the case of *viejo/a*, when **estar** is employed, the emphasis is placed on the person's state—the way the person is behaving or acting, albeit permanently. The statement:

María siempre *está* cariñosa

does not explicitly define her nature. In fact, it could even mean (though not necessarily) that Maria's nature is not affectionate but that, perhaps through her incredibly strong willpower, she is always able to make the effort to behave in an amiable and affectionate manner. Of course, it could be the case that Maria is in fact a naturally affectionate person. However, this statement does not necessarily imply this. Having opted not to use *ser*, the phrase does not explicitly commit itself to the concept of what Maria is or is not by nature. The choice of **estar** rather than *ser* clearly denotes the speaker's intended meaning or emphasis as being that of **HOWNESS.**

If we now turn to the statement:

María siempre *es* cariñosa

in order to understand the meaning of this, it will probably help if we start by breaking the phrase down slightly.

We will begin by taking out the word '*siempre*' and simply say that *María es cariñosa*. By now, you will be aware that this expression indicates that Maria is a naturally affectionate kind of person. This could even mean that though Maria is affectionate by nature, she may not always act affectionately (perhaps owing to some sad event or circumstances beyond her control which affect her demeanour, and thus on occasions make her seem uncharacteristically distant). These circumstantial events, however, do not affect her true nature.

Now, we will put back the word *'siempre'* and say *María siempre es cariñosa*. The addition of 'siempre' to the phrase compliments and modifies the verb (in this case, by extending its meaning). The phrase *María siempre es cariñosa* therefore not only explicitly indicates **WHAT** Maria is: she is affectionate by nature. It now tells us that in addition to being a naturally affectionate person, she also always (*siempre*) acts in that way. It informs us as to her nature **and** her behaviour.

A short-cut to knowing how to choose between *ser* and *estar* is to remember that:

1. *SER* is used whenever your intended meaning is that of **WHATNESS,** rather than HOWNESS, and the phrase used is a short (elliptical) version of:

Someone is **a/an** something:

Pedro is **an** old man

Carmen is **a** spinster

For instance:

*Es soltera = Es [**una persona**] soltera*
She is a spinster

Es divorciada = *Es [una persona]* divorciada.
She is a divorcee

Es cariñoso = *Es [una persona]* cariñosa
He is **an** affectionate person
(*He is* **an** *affectionate* **sort of** *person*)

2. *ESTAR* is used whenever your intended meaning is merely that
of **HOWNESS** (including marital status).

For instance:

Está soltera — She is single

Está divorciada — She is divorced

Está cariñoso — He is affectionate.
(i.e. He is behaving affectionately)

2. AN INFORMED CHOICE

Understanding the options offered to you in the use of *ser* and
estar with qualifying adjectives is an instance which clearly
illustrates what we said at the outset, i.e., that it is not until the
underlying meaning is understood that this creative and effective
use of language can begin.

Ser or *Estar*—and the Art of the Back-handed Compliment

As an example of the effective use of *ser* and *estar*, let us take the
adjectives *inteligente* (intelligent). Students are often taught that this

word is one in that long list of exceptions which should only take *ser*, as for instance:

Ricardo *es* inteligente.

In fact, the word *inteligente* can also be used very effectively with *estar*. But when so used, the result can easily be either an openly sarcastic remark or a nicely disguised insult. For by the very use of *estar* in this phrase we are explicitly limiting Ricardo's intelligence to a particular accidental instance and thus denying Ricardo (by not using the verb *ser*) the quality of intelligence as a natural or inherent characteristic. We could even be implying that Ricardo is not very bright, but has just, accidentally, shown a bit of intelligence for the first time in his life.

Whereas when the verb *ser* is used in the phrase *Ricardo **es** inteligente*, we now know that we are saying: *Ricardo es **una persona** inteligente*. (Ricardo is an intelligent person), i.e.:

Ricardo = inteligente

Employing *estar* instead of *ser*, would therefore mean that we are not signalling the above equation, rather we are making the question of Ricardo's natural intelligence the subject of doubt and speculation.

You will now appreciate how the incorrect use of *ser* and *estar* can result in some embarrassing, difficult, or precarious situations, which can get one into very hot water.

This was the case of the student who was so enthusiastic about his progress in Spanish and the ability of his teacher that he went around informing his Spanish friends:

Mi profesor *está* muy bueno

believing that with this phrase he was saying 'My teacher is very good.' It was not until he had repeated this a few times and noticed the reactions and strange comments he was getting—comments such as: *¿Cómo lo sabes?* (How do you know?)—that he realized he was using the wrong 'to be' verb, and should have said:

Mi profesor *es* muy bueno

What he was in fact expressing with the phrase *Mi profesor **está** muy bueno* (a colloquial expression charged with sexual innuendo) was: 'My teacher is hot stuff/a pretty hot dish'.* This sort of mistake is one of the commonest to be heard from learners of Spanish.

Understanding the fundamental principle behind the use of these verbs gives you the advantage of being able to make an informed choice. A thorough knowledge and awareness of the way *ser* and *estar* function will also be a major asset in the use and appreciation of humour—the humour which can result from purposely interchanging or skilfully playing around with these verbs.

Instances of this are numerous. One that occurred to a colleague, a Spanish professor talking to a group of nuns about the Pope's tiring work schedule and his lack of sleep, was:

...el Papa se acuesta tan tarde que no *está* muy católico

---

* For further discussion of *estar* as HOWNESS with sexual connotations see p. 57.

Several of the nuns, who obviously did not understand the difference between *ser* and *estar,* misinterpreted the comment and thought he had said that, as the Pope goes to bed so late (*el Papa se acuesta tan tarde*), he is not a good Catholic. This, of course, would have been the case had the professor used *ser* and not *estar.* But the word *católico* when used with *estar* refers to a person's state of health. Thus his remark that the Pope "*no está muy católico*" was a light-hearted comment, playing on words, and simply meant that the Pope was not very well.

Knowing how to use these verbs accurately can also mean the difference between cracking a subtle joke and putting your foot in it through ignorance. This latter was the case of the man who, when talking about the incredible wealth of his rather elderly male boss, said:

Mi jefe *está* rico con ganas

instead of:

Mi jefe *es* rico con ganas

When he saw the reaction of his friends, who fell about laughing, he realized that he had said the wrong thing. Having used *estar* rather than *ser,* instead of saying 'My boss is very rich', what he had actually said was: 'My boss is very delicious/dishy'. You might indeed say this about a plate of exquisite food but not about a person—unless, of course, you are purposely playing around with words and want to say that the person concerned is good enough to eat.

Being aware of the distinction between *ser* and *estar* will help you avoid making mistakes unwittingly—making what could be insulting, offensive, or just amusing remarks unintentionally, merely by using the wrong verb.

41

This knowledge will also lead to the sort of command of the language which will help you communicate successfully. It will mean that on the rare (we hope) occasions when you want to insult someone, you will do this effectively. You will know how to insult openly, if this is what you want to do. More importantly, perhaps, you will know how to avoid this, if it is not your intention to offend. You will be aware of disguised insults or back-handed compliments, as reflected in the above phrase *Ricardo está inteligente*.

When an open insult is called for, rather than one of ironic subtlety, the verb *ser* is used with negative qualities. So, that, if we wanted to say quite openly and barely that Ricardo is a stupid person, we would say in Spanish:

Ricardo *es* estúpido.

And even if we did not genuinely believe that Ricardo is truly *estúpido* (stupid), in a moment of anger we feel this with such passion and conviction that we say it **as though we really meant it.** Besides, if we said *Ricardo está estúpido* it would not be a real insult, or at best, it would only be a very weak one.

Conversely, with the earlier-mentioned phrase *Juan está siempre preocupado* (Juan is always worried/in a worried state.), here *estar* is used precisely so as not to offend Juan by converting his negative state into an intrinsic or pathological condition. By choosing *estar* rather than *ser*, it is only his state of being or manner of behaving (albeit permanent) which is being emphasized. There is no explicit reference to his natural characteristics.

Ser or *Estar*—and your Intended Meaning

The next two examples of *ser* and *estar* used with the qualifying adjectives *alto/a* (tall) and *guapo/a* (beautiful) will further help you appreciate how these verbs function and illustrate how your intended meaning is governed by an informed choice.

(SER)   **(ESTAR)**

Mi hijo *es* alto   **Mi hijo *está* alto**

In the case where **ser** is used, *Mi hijo es alto.* (My son is tall), the father sees the son's tallness as an essential, defining characteristic of his person. When making this statement the father is leaving no room for doubt: the son is tall according to the way in which he understands tallness in a boy. It is an objective observation which identifies the son as a tall boy.

Whereas in the case where **estar** is used, *Mi hijo está alto* (My son is/appears tall), the father is not making an observation with which he necessarily expects everyone to agree, nor is he emphasizing a quality in the son which he considers to be an inherent attribute. The emphasis is on the state the son is in now. It is a subjective observation, perhaps indicating a sudden or considerable **change** (i.e. since the son's last birthday, or perhaps the father has been away for a while and on his return finds that his son has shot up in height since he last saw him). This observation is thus limited to these particular and implicit circumstances—and these are revealed precisely by the use of *estar.*

Taking the adjective *guapo/a* as a second example, when talking about María it is possible to say, for instance:

(SER)	(ESTAR)
María es guapa	**María está guapa**

In the case where *ser* is used, *María es guapa* (María is beautiful), here the emphasis is placed on *guapa* as something which is natural attribute of María. At least, the person who is making the statement believes it to be so and this belief is expressed unreservedly. That is to say, this conception that María is beautiful is held with such conviction that the person making the statement cannot conceive of María without this attribute of beauty: María is beautiful by nature, even if, due to some unfortunate, accidental, circumstance like illness, she does not look too good at present, and thus does not always appear *guapa*. (This is also another example which challenges the idea that *ser* can always be associated with permanence or immutability.)

However, in the case where ***estar*** is used, *María está guapa* (María looks beautiful*), the statement merely emphasizes **HOW** María appears now. Thus this statement could even mean that in fact

---

* Although the literal translation of this phrase would be 'María is beautiful', a more accurate translation would be 'María looks beautiful'. It seems that, in this case, it is important to make the intended circumstantial meaning explicit even in English. For this reason, the all-purpose verb 'to be' is here rendered inadequate and another verb must be employed to avoid ambiguity and to render explicit the meaning conveyed by the Spanish verb *estar*.

María is not naturally very good looking, but in the present circumstances—perhaps because she has made a special effort to dress elegantly, is wearing make-up or has had her hair done, etc.—she looks good now. The emphasis is therefore only on her physical state/appearance in these circumstances. In this case, the idea that *estar* signifies transitory conditions may help some students. Nevertheless, we believe that from the outset it is much better for you to be aware of the real, fundamental, difference between *ser* and *estar*—that of **WHATNESS** and **HOWNESS.**

* * *

The application of this principle could be especially helpful to learners faced, for instance, with the choice of which of the verbs to use when talking about food and drink.

Many learners seem to find this rather tricky. This could be due in some measure to the colloquial manner in which the English verb 'to be' is often employed in such cases. It is a particularly graphic example of where, in English, context and/or intonation play an important role in helping to reveal the intended meaning.

If, for instance, we take the bare question:

What is the meat/wine like?

as it stands, this phrase is ambiguous and could have several meanings. So the first step is to be aware of the sense you want to convey when using this very serviceable, multi-purpose phrase. It is only when this has been done, that you will be in a position to formulate a question which will correctly convey this meaning in Spanish. Two of the most obvious meanings are:

1) **'What is the meat/wine like?'** could refer to the natural qualities or characteristics of the meat or wine. In this sense, the questioner would be expecting an objective response that would define these inherent attributes. In the case of the meat, the question could refer to whether it was tender, juicy, lean, fatty, etc. In the case of the wine, it could refer to whether it was full-bodied, fruity, strong, earthy, or other such defining characteristics.

2) **'What is the meat/wine like?'** could also be asking about the state the meat/wine is in—whether it was in good or bad condition at a particular time.

Clearly, in 1) the intended meaning is that of **WHATNESS.** And in Spanish, as we have seen, this would be explicitly indicated by using the verb *ser* to formulate the question:

¿Cómo *es* la carne/el vino?

Whereas, in 2) the intended meaning is that of **HOWNESS**—even though in English the question is formulated rather imprecisely with the word 'what', it is in fact not a WHAT question, but one referring to state/condition. Hence the equivalent formulation of Spanish would require *estar:*

¿Cómo *está* la carne/el vino?

The question 'What is the meat/wine like?' could also be a colloquial way of asking as to whether or not the meat/wine is to your liking.

Here, it would be a question calling for your subjective opinion on the meat/wine—whether, by your standards, you would say it was good, bad, nice, indifferent, etc. Of course, there are many other ways of asking such a question. But if you want to use the verb 'to be', then in Spanish the question would have to be formulated with *estar,* as the intended meaning is again one of **HOWNESS.** It is an enquiry as to HOW you personally find the meat/wine—are they to your taste or liking?

You will realize, therefore, that it is important to be clear about your intended meaning in order to be able to formulate the question correctly in Spanish.

A short-cut to remembering which of these verbs to use with adjectives can be found in the formulation of the following two questions:

¿**Cómo** *es* **alguien/algo?** = **WHAT** is someone/something like?

¿**Cómo** *está* **alguien/algo?** = **HOW** is someone/something?

As you can see, the only difference in the way these two questions are formulated is that the first one uses *ser* and the second *estar.* Both questions use the same question word (¿*Cómo?*). However, when ¿*Cómo?* is used with *ser* it means **WHAT,** whereas when used with *estar* it means **HOW.** So that the choice as to whether you use *ser* or *estar* with *¿Cómo?* will depend on which of two very different questions you want to ask:

If you ask *¿Cómo es Juan?* (What is Juan like?) or *¿Cómo es el vino?* (What is the wine like?), it is clear that you are asking for information about some of those inherent or essential qualities which serve to describe the nature or identity of the person or thing concerned. Whereas if you ask *¿Cómo está Juan?* (How is Juan?) or *¿Cómo está el vino?* (How is the wine?), you are asking about the state of being or condition of the person or thing concerned at a particular time. Once again, these two examples bring us back, quite literally, to the basic, fundamental, difference between *ser* and *estar*, which is that of:

WHATNESS AND HOWNESS

Furthermore, this main difference holds true for all qualifying adjectives. And although in some cases (as in *María siempre es/está cariñosa*) for all practical purposes this difference might appear minor or even negligible, in most cases it is in fact quite obvious and major. But whether major or minor in scope or intensity, the difference is always the same in kind.

CHAPTER THREE

Beyond the Rules

III

NOT MANY RULES— BUT *ONE* MAIN PRINCIPLE

We mentioned earlier that most grammar books set out lists of rules showing when to use *ser* or *estar*. Yet, you have seen in the examples dealt with so far that each of these cases is governed by the same fundamental principle outlined in the previous chapters. There are, in fact, no independent, unconnected rules which have to be learnt by rote, and this holds true for all cases, including the so-called 'exceptions'. It will serve no purpose, therefore, simply to restate here every one of the indicated uses of *ser* and *estar* to be found in the many available books on the Spanish language. It will be much more profitable if we focus on them in order to make transparent exactly why and how they are all covered by the basic principle of **Whatness** and **Howness.** For only when this is understood will the learner at last have a firm grasp of the way these key verbs function.

Whatness *versus* Howness

First, a reminder of the main hints mentioned earlier:

Ser = WHATNESS

It is used when we want to:

> 1) define WHAT someone or something is;
>
> 2) indicate the essential characteristics
> of someone or something: say WHAT
> he/she/it is like;
>
> 3) identify WHO someone is (WHAT is
> the identity of that person).

Estar = HOWNESS

It is used when we want to:

> 1) refer to the particular STATE of a person
> or thing, whether this be permanent or temporary;
>
> 2) refer to marital status: HOW someone stands
> marriage-wise;
>
> 3) refer to position/location: HOW something/
> someone is situated, either in a literal or figurative sense.

I.I *Ser* = WHATNESS

Defining:

Nature	*¿Qué es?* —	What is he/she/it?
Character	*¿Cómo es?* —	What is he/she/it like
Physical characteristics		
Identity	*¿Quién es?* —	Who is he/she?
		(What is the identity of)

NATURE:
Es un árbol
(It is a tree)

CHARACTER:
— Inherent qualities:
Luis es amable
Luis es [una persona] amable
(Luis is kind)

— Inherent moral characteristics:
Ana es buena
Ana es [una persona] buena
(Ana is a good person)

— Inherent intellectual
characteristics:
Carmen es inteligente
(Carmen is intelligent)

PHYSICAL CHARACTERISTICS:
Alfonso es alto
(Alfonso is tall)

IDENTITY:
Es María Enríquez
(It is María Enríquez)

I.2 *Estar* = HOWNESS

Denoting:

— Physical State:
  health
  mood   *¿Cómo está?*   —   How is he/she?
  appearance
  behaviour, etc.

— Marital Status: ***Estar*** *soltero/a* — To be single
                       casado/a   married

— Location: *¿Dónde estás?* — Where are you?

PHYSICAL STATE:

— Health: *Ana **está** bien*
             (Ana is well/in good physical condition)

— Mood: *Juan **está** triste*
                           (Juan is sad)

— Health or mood: ***Estoy*** *fatal*
                           (I feel rotten)

— Appearance: ***Estás*** *elegante hoy*
                  (You look elegant today)

— Behaviour: *José **está** cariñoso*
                   (José is affectionate)

MARITAL STATUS: ***Estoy*** *divorciado*
                     (I am divorced)

LOCATION: *Juan y Pili **están** en Madrid*
                        (Juan and Pili are in
                                  Madrid)

Estar Indicating State of Health or Comfort: A Miniature Case Study
Mal, Malo/a, Bien, Bueno/a

1. *Mal*

The adverb *mal* can be used with *estar* (often found in colloquial phrases) when referring to people, as for example:

¡Tú estás mal!
(You are in a bad way!)
(You are not functioning well)

Depending on the context, *estar mal* could mean to be ill or 'off' (either physically or mentally); to be tired, under the weather, etc.

2. *Malo/a*

The adjective *malo/a* when used with *estar* refers to the state of health:

Jaime está malo
(Jaime is ill)

3. *Bien*

When *estar* is used with the adverb *bien* (well), it indicates state of health or comfort:

Jaime está bien
(Jaime is well/in good physical condition)

¿Estás bien?
(Are you comfortable/all right?)

4. Bueno/a

Note that the adjective *bueno/a* is not usually used with *estar* when referring to the physical state of people as this can have sexual connotations.

> *Mi jefe está bueno*
> (My boss is hot stuff/a hot dish)

This is so because the inference here is that the person concerned is 'in a good state for ...'—*está bueno para* ... (See also Warning Section below.)

Nevertheless, you will often hear phrases like:

> *Elena ya está buena*

indicating that 'Elena is now well/healthy, i.e., the word *ya* (now) implies that the statement is made in a context within which it is clear that earlier Elena had been ill, and in such a context the phrase would not have any untoward meaning.

Notice also that the adjective *bueno/a* presents no problems when used with *estar* to refer to the state or condition of things. We saw this in the example cited in chapter two:

> *El vino está bueno*
> (The wine is good/to my taste/ in a good state)

WARNING!

HOWNESS and Sexual Connotations

As in other languages there are colloquial phrases in Spanish which have clear sexual allusions. Many of these are created (as we saw in the case of *bueno/a* above) by employing *estar* so as to empasize the sexual state at a particular time.

1. *Caliente, frío/a*

The adjectives *caliente* (hot) and *frío/a* are not normally used with *estar* when referring to the state of a person (or, at least, they are only used in circumstances of familiarity) as this could result in offensive remarks or embarrassing situations. This is very similar to the way the words hot and cold can be interpreted in English in certain contexts.

> *Felipe está caliente* = Felipe is feeling hot (sexually)

> *Clara está fría* = Clara is cold (frigid)

But:

> *El café está caliente* = The coffee is hot

> *La sopa está fría* = The soup is cold

2. *Salido/a*
Cachondo/a

Although these words do not come under the heading of so-called obscene or swear words, when used with *estar* they do result in rather strong expressions that many would find offensive. Care should therefore be taken both in the context and company in which such expressions are used.

Estar salido/a
Estar cachondo/a
(To be or feel horny/randy/sexy)

The use of *salido/a* here is derived from its original reference to the periodic state of animals in the breeding season or, colloquially, 'on heat'. Similarly *cachondo/a* was originally used to refer specifically to the state of a bitch on heat, but its figurative use has been extended to people.

Nowadays, however, *cachondo/a* is often used with *ser* to identify someone of waggish disposition or an extrovert. So that more and more one can encounters the expression:

Es un cachondo/a

indicating a person who has a natural propensity for telling jokes or fooling around.

NOTE

> As in other languages, colloquial expressions are often the victims of fashion. They can also vary according to region and their meanings sometimes undergo change with the passage of time.

It is interesting to see how a clear understanding of the way *ser* and *estar* function immediately illuminates many expressions that were previously perceived as being arbitrarily constructed and capricious—and which it was thought just had to be learned by rote along with many other colloquial expressions. If we take as an example just one of these cases—*ser* and *estar* used with *perdido/a* (lost)—you will see that these expressions are not without logic. They are rooted in the principle of WHATNESS and HOWNESS and this sheds light even on the figurative or colloquial use of words:

HOWNESS:

Estar perdido/a
(To be lost/to lose one's way)

WHATNESS:

Ser *[una] perdida*
(To be a lost woman/a loose woman/a harlot)

Ser *[un] perdido*
(To be a lost man/a libertine/dissolute person)

You will now appreciate how not being aware of the distinction between *ser* and *estar* can lead to perplexing, troublesome or funny situations. Such was the case of the young woman tourist who brought a smile to the faces of passengers on a crowded bus in Madrid. Having taken a *No.7* instead of a *No.9* bus, she suddenly realized that she was lost and jumped up exclaiming: *¡Soy perdida, muy perdida!*

The Principle Underlying the Rules

WHATNESS — *Ser* Denoting Identity:

— Profession
— Rank   *¿Qué es?*   What is he/she?
— Religion   *Alguien es* ... — Someone is a ...
— Nationality
— Origin

PROFESSION: *Juan es médico*
Juan es [un] médico
(Juan is a doctor)

RANK: *Carlos es teniente*
Carlos es [un] teniente
(Carlos is a lieutenant)

RELIGION: *Ana es católica*
Ana es [una] católica
Ana es [una persona] católica
(Ana is a catholic)

NATIONALITY: *John es inglés*
John es [un] inglés
John es [un hombre] inglés
(John is English/is an Englishman)

ORIGIN: *Sara es de España*
Sara es [natural/una persona] de España
(Sara is from Spain)

The expression **ser de** does not, in fact, refer to position or state. It identifies origin and nationality in the sense of being 'a native of' *(natural de)* and thus denotes WHATNESS: **Soy de** *Yorkshire* = I am from/a native of Yorkshire; I am a Yorkshireman/woman

HOWNESS—*Estar* Indicating:

1. Acting as/Working in the capacity of/Temporarily employed as:

   Estoy de *director*
   (I am acting as manager)

2. Temporary activity:

   Estoy de *viaje*
   (I am travelling)

3. Behaving in a certain manner/Feeling like/Mood/Giving the appearance of (figuratively or literally):

   Estoy de *broma*
   (I am in a joking mood)

   Juan ***está*** *tonto*
   (Juan is behaving like a fool)

---

1. a) ACTING AS, etc.
(Profession and Employment):

Estar can be used with professions. When used in this way it does not refer to what the person is but HOW they are situated at the present time, i.e., working in a particular capacity, temporarily employed as, etc.. In these cases the verb is followed by the preposition ***de—estar de:***

José ***está de*** *médico en el hospital San Carlos*

The emphasis here is either on the place where José is working (location) or on the temporary nature of the job he is doing. What this phrase actually means is: *José está [ejerciendo su profesión] de médico en el hospital de San Carlos* = José is practicing as a a doctor (either permanently or temporarily) at the San Carlos Hospital.

Similarly, the phrase:

Fernando está de cartero
Fernando está [trabajando] de cartero
(Fernando is working as a postman)

You will see that this phrase does not necessarily indicate that Fernando is 'a something'—a postman. It merely informs us that he is working in this capacity at the moment. Fernando might be a student who is working as a postman during the vacation. Thus, the phrase does not tell us WHAT he is, but HOW he is currently working. The emphasis is on his present situation.

1. b) ACTING AS, etc.
(Colloquial and Figurative Expressions):

There are also colloquial and figurative expressions using words which normally indicate rank, religion or nationality, but which, when used with *estar*, take on different meanings. For instance:

Teniente

In Spain lieutenants *(tenientes)* had a reputation for being either deaf or mean—or both. Hence the colloquial expression:

¡*Estás teniente!*
(You are tight-fisted!)

¿*Estás teniente?*
(Are you deaf/hard of hearing?)

62

— *Católico/a*

We saw in the previous chapter that the word *católico/a* when used with *estar* does not refer to a person's religion, but indicates a state of health. It can also denote behaviour. In Spanish culture the word *católico/a* has through the ages always been associated with all that was good, acceptable, orthodox, sound, right. Hence:

No estoy muy católico/a
(I am not feeling very well)
(I am out of sorts)

Estás de un católico
(You are behaving/acting in a dogmatic/intransigent manner)

— **Adjectives of nationality:**

When adjectives of nationality are employed with **estar** or **estar de** the resulting phrase indicates behaviour or appearance:

Estás muy inglés
¡Estás de un inglés!
(You look/are behaving like a true Englishman)

2. TEMPORARY ACTIVITY:

Estoy de mudanza
(I am in the middle of moving house)

Estoy de vacaciones
(I am on holiday)

Estar de charla
(To have a chat)

3. APPEARING LIKE/BEHAVING LIKE/MOOD, etc.:

Appearing like:

> *Estás de un elegante*
> (You are so smart/elegant)

Meaning

> *Estás [vestido] de [un modo tan] elegante*
> (You are dressed so smartly)

Behaving like:

> *Estás de un estúpido*
> (You are so stupid)

Meaning:

> *Estás [comportándote] de [un modo tan] estúpido*
> (You are behaving in such a stupid way)

Mood:

> *Estás de buen/mal humor*
> (You are in a good/bad mood)

And so on with numerous other examples.

It should now be clear that in such expressions indicating behaviour, mood, temporary activity, etc., *estar* is used as they all have as their common denominator the basic principle of HOW-NESS. That is to say, they all refer to the situation or state a person is in—either mentally or physically, figuratively or literally.

WHATNESS—*Ser* **Denoting:**

— Origin/Material: *¿De qué es?*   *Es de oro*
                   (What is it made of?) (It is a gold object)

— Ownership: *¿De quién es?*   *Es de María*
                     (Whose is it?)   (It is María's)

ORIGIN/MATERIAL:
— Denoting WHAT something is made of:
         Es de plata
         Es [un objeto] de plata
         (It is a silver object)

         El vestido es de seda
         (It is a silk dress)
         (lit. The dress is of silk)

OWNERSHIP:

— Identifying something as being the property of someone:

         De María, de Juan, etc.
         (Mary's, John's etc.)
         mío/a, tuyo/a, etc.
         (mine/your, etc.)

         Es el libro de Juan
         (It is John's book)
         Es de Juan
         (It's John's)

         El coche es mío
         (The car is mine)

Identifying by Equating

To identify by equating one thing with another —

Ser is used:

— Before nouns	*Es el director*
	(He is the manager)
— Before pronouns	*Es éste*
	(It is this one)
— In generalizations	*El dinero es peligroso*
	(Money is dangerous)
— In impersonal expressions	*Es importante que...*
	(It is important that...)
— With infinitives	*Meditar es rezar*
	(To meditate is to pray)

Ser **before nouns:**

We have already seen the way in which *ser* is used before a noun (and noun phrases) to denote WHAT someone or something is. In such constructions the verb serves to link, identify or equate one thing with another:

Hoy es fiesta
Hoy = fiesta
Hoy es [un día de] fiesta
(Today is a holiday)

María es profesora de español
María es [una] profesora de español
(Maria is a Spanish teacher)

Es un ladrón
(He is a thief)

Ser before pronouns:

This construction of *ser* before a pronoun (a word which replaces a noun) also defines identity by equating one thing with another:

Hoy día un dólar no es nada
Un dólar = nada
(These days a dollar is nothing)

Algo es algo
(Something is better than nothing)
(lit. Something is something)

Mi casa es ésa
(My house is that one)

Ser with generalizations:

A generalization is the classification or reduction of particulars (people, things or ideas) under one general heading or rule. It constitutes a factual, inductive, or objective statement informing us as to WHAT someone or something is, to which group they belong, etc. :

El hombre es un animal racional
(Man is a rational animal)

El agua es esencial para la vida
(Water is essential for life)

La belleza es eterna
(Beauty is eternal)

El tiempo es oro
(Time is money)
(lit. Time is gold)

Ser with impersonal expressions:

These cases are very similar to the use of *ser* in generalizations. They take the form of factual, objective, or inductive statements, in which *ser* is used in an impersonal manner:

Es normal que...	—	It is normal that...
Es necesario que...	—	It is necessary that...
Es evidente/cierto que...	—	It is evident/certain that...
Es claro que*...	—	It is clear that...

Such expressions indicate WHAT it is that is clear, normal, necessary, evident, etc.

Ser with infinitives:

This formulation (infinitive + *ser*) is used to classify particular actions or ideas so as to bring them under one general heading, rule or statement. Once more, these constructions take the form of generalizations or abstractions, and *ser* is used here to equate one thing or idea with another:

Fumar es malo

Fumar = malo
(Smoking is bad)

Fumar es [un hábito] malo
(Smoking is a bad habit)

---

* Rarely used, see p. 70 for explanation of **ser** *claro* and **estar** *claro*.

In such phrases the infinitive (*fumar* in the above phrase) is here converted into a sort of noun—*el fumar*—though the definite article (*el*) is omitted in an ellipsis. When translated into English, this is sometimes dealt with by using a gerund (a gerund is formed by adding **-ing** to a verb). Here *fumar* or *el fumar* would be equivalent to the English 'smoking'. A complete version of the doubly elliptical phrase *fumar es malo* would be:

[El] fumar es [un hábito] malo

Likewise, with other similar generalizations or phrases expressing abstract ideas. For instance:

Amar es comprender
(Loving is understanding)

Ver es creer
(Seeing is believing)

BUT:

There are often better, more idiomatic ways of translating such constructions, e.g. :

Querer es poder
(Where there's a will, there's a way)

¿*Es o Está claro?*

Estar claro que...

Although, technically speaking, the adjective *claro* may be used almost indistinctly with both *ser* and *estar,* in fact the expression *estar claro que...* seems to have supplanted *ser claro que...* (which is rarely heard nowadays) in everyday use.

We saw in the previous section dealing with *ser* that expressions such as *es claro/evidente que...* etc., indicate factual, objective, or inductive observations.

However, when using *estar,* it is not the notion of objectivity , the unquestionable or factual nature of the statement that is being emphasized, but rather the personal judgment or circumstantial context. The stress is on one's opinion or perception of the situation—HOW it appears—on the evidence to hand at the time. As this emphasis is the one most frequently intended, *está claro que...* is the idiom most often used. For instance, in the phrase:

Está claro que ya no viene
(It's clear that he is not coming now)

what is meant is that on the evidence to hand this is my impression or opinion, i.e. that he will not come now. Likewise, in the phrase:

Está claro que no estudia nada
(Its clear that he does not study at all)

by using *estar* we are implicitly emphasizing the subjective nature of the statement, and thus the phrase *Está claro que no estudia nada* means that It's clear [to me] that he does not study at all.

70

Estar as a Synonym

Estar as a synonym of verbs referring to the situation/position someone or something is in:

— *hallarse*
— *encontrarse*
— *quedarse*
— *verse*
— *andar*

Estar is often used as a synonym of:

1. *hallarse/encontrarse:*

(literally meaning to find oneself in a position of)

Hallarse/Encontrarse enfermo = ***Estar*** *enfermo*
(To be ill)

Hallarse/Encontrarse sin dinero = ***Estar*** *sin dinero*
(To find oneself without money)

2. *quedarse:*

(literally: to remain, to stay, to stay on)

Quedarse embarazada = ***Estar*** *embarazada*
(To be pregnant)

Quedarse en Babia = ***Estar*** *en Babia*
(To be daydreaming)

3. *verse:*

(lit. to see oneself; fig. to find oneself)

Verse en un aprieto = **Estar** *en un aprieto*
(To be in a fix)

Verse sin trabajo = **Estar** *sin trabajo*
(To be without work)

4. *andar:*

(lit. to walk; fig. to find oneself)

¿Cómo andas? = *¿Cómo* **estás?**
(How are you?)

Ando preocupado = **Estoy** *preocupado*
(I am worried)

Estar with Prepositions

Indicating the relationship of people and things in space and time
—HOW someone or something is situated, feeling, looking etc.

Estar a :

Estar *a punto de*
(To be on the point of)

Todavía **estás a** *tiempo*
(You've still got time)
(lit. Still you are in time)

Estar con:

Estar con *dolor de cabeza*
(To have a headache)
(lit. To be with a headache)

Estar con *mal aspecto*
(To look ill/off)

Estar de:

Estar de *pie*
(To be standing)

Estar de *vuelta*
(To be back)

Estar en:

Estar en *cuclillas*
(To be in a squatting position)

Estar en guardia
(To be on guard)

Estar entre:

Estar entre la vida y la muerte
(To be at death's door)
(lit. To be between life and death)

Estar para:

Estoy para salir
(I'm about to /ready to go out, I'm on the point of leaving)

No *estoy* para bromas
(I am in no mood for jokes)

Estar por:

Estoy por salir
(I am tempted to go out /thinking of leaving)

Está por ver
(It remains to be seen)

Estar sobre:

Estar sobre aviso
(To be on the alert)

Estar sobre ascuas
(To be on tenterhooks)
(lit. To be on hot coals)

Estar + preposition + *Fiesta*

A Miniature Case-Study:

The word *fiesta* used with different prepositions

You will notice that, though the following expressions have different nuances, the use of *estar* indicates that they will always denote HOWNESS in some way, i.e., state, situation or position (either literally or figuratively).

Estar de fiesta — to be celebrating

Estar de fiestas — to be in high spirits/ good humour

Estar en fiestas — to be en fête (indicating a local or national holiday/festival)

No estar para fiestas — to be in no mood for jokes.

Ser and *Estar* with Dates

This is a case where the difference between *ser* and *estar* seems negligible and where the expressions are practically interchangeable. However, there is still a difference in emphasis and nuance. With *estar* the emphasis is once more one of situation. *Estar* specifically refers to HOW someone is placed in time. Whereas, the phrases using *ser* are totally impersonal. They denote WHATNESS and serve only to identify the day, the date. For instance:

Es domingo
(It is Sunday)

You will notice, however, that those phrases employing *estar* personalize the situation. They do not say 'it is Sunday', but literally 'we are at Sunday':

Estamos a domingo

Furthermore, when referring to dates, it is not possible to use *estar* in an impersonal manner and say '*está domingo*'. Conversely, with *ser* it is not possible to personalize the situation by saying '*somos a domingo*'. In this way, *estar* once again indicates HOWNESS; here it situates people (**us**—*nosotros*) in a particular time. The problem for the English speaker is that, though in Spanish the meaning is clear, in this particular instance the English language is not rich enough to render this adequately. There is no expression which can convey the subtle difference between the Whatness and the Howness of *ser* and *estar* used with dates. Consequently, this is lost in translation.

Note:
In order to give the English speaker a better understanding of the meaning conveyed by the use of *estar* with dates, it might help if

a parallel is drawn with the way 'to be' is used in English when referring to time in the colloquial expression 'How are we for time?', (i.e. 'How are we [fixed] for time?'). The emphasis here is not on the time itself, but HOW the time affects us. The same is true of *estar* used in the above cases with dates.

Dates:

Ser = WHATNESS	*Estar* = HOWNESS
Denoting identity	Referring to a situation within a particular time and space. It has a specific reference to WHERE/HOW **we** are situated date-wise.
¿Qué día es hoy? (What day is it today?)	*¿A qué día estamos?* (What day is it today?)
Hoy es domingo (Today is Sunday)	*Estamos a domingo* (Today is Sunday)
¿Qué fecha es hoy? (What is the date today?)	*¿A cuántos estamos?* (What's the date today?)
Hoy *es [el] seis de junio...* (Today is the sixth of June...)	Hoy *estamos a seis de junio...* (Today is the six of June...)

Ser and *Estar* with Past Participles

Both verbs can be used with the past participle.

First a reminder:

In Spanish the past participle is formed by adding:

> **-ado** to the stem of *-ar* verbs;

> **-ido** to the stem of *-er* and *-ir* verbs.

In English this often corresponds to the endings **ed/en,** e.g. lived, spoken, etc. (But of course, there are irregular past participles both in English and Spanish.)

Trabajar (to work)	—	trabaj**ado** (worked)
Hablar (to speak)	—	habl**ado** (spoken)
Comer (to eat)	—	com**ido** (eaten)
Beber (to drink)	—	beb**ido** (drunk)
Vivir (to live)	—	viv**ido** (lived)
Pedir (to ask for)	—	ped**ido** (asked for)

When the past participle is used with *ser* or *estar* its ending must agree in gender and number with the subject:

La señora es/está casada	— The woman is married
Las señoras son/están casadas	— The women are married
El niño es amado por sus padres	— The child is loved by his parents
Los niños son amados por sus padres	— The children are loved by their parents

1) *Ser* with Past Participles

Ser is used with the past participle to form the passive voice. Before we go on, it might prove worthwhile to take a quick look at the difference between the passive and active voices:

When referring to actions or states, we can often express what is taking place in two different ways. The most usual way in both English and Spanish (but even more so in Spanish) is to use the active voice. That is to say, when talking about, say, John doing some work, we could say:

John does the work

This takes the form of the construction:

A does **B**
A (John) does **B** (the work)

We could also express this idea by inverting the above phrase and saying **B** is done by **A**:

The work is done by John
B (the work) is done by **A** (John)

This latter is the passive voice. It is used when:

1) the agent, or doer of the action, is of less importance than what is being done;

2) what is being done is of primary importance and we either do not know, or do not want to say, who the doer is.

Active: Maria closes the door slowly

Passive 1):   The door is closed slowly by Maria
Passive 2):   The door is closed slowly

In Spanish, the passive voice is used with *ser* and it indicates what is, has been or will be done, etc.

> *La puerta es cerrada despacio por María*
> (The door is closed slowly by Maria)

One of the difficulties encountered by learners is due to the fact that they are often unaware that the passive is sometimes elliptical - the past participle is often omitted (as we shall see below.) However, though omitted, the past participle remains implicit in the phrase. Confusion then arises between this shortened, or elliptical, passive and the way *estar* is used in the active voice in phrases which indicate situation or location. Such confusion causes many to wring their hands in frustration when trying to grapple with what they believe is the impossible task of finding any logical basis for these seemingly capricious linguistic structures. For example:

> A) *La clase es en el quinto piso*

and

> B) *La clase está en el quinto piso*

However, once you know that the first phrase is an elliptical form of the passive sentence:

> *La clase es [celebrada] en el quinto piso*
> (The lesson/class is [being held] on the fifth floor)

you will realize that here the thing being emphasized is what is happening on the 5th floor. Whereas in the phrase formulated with *estar:*

*La clase **está** en el quinto piso*
(The classroom is on the fifth floor)

the emphasis is on Whereness—HOW/WHERE a person or thing (in this case the classroom) is located. This particular case is further complicated by the fact that the word *clase* can have several meanings, e.g., lesson, class (group of students), class (type), classroom.

The practical difference between the use of the active and passive here may seem negligible and we do not wish to imply that it is greater than it actually is. However, there is a difference and this difference is logical.

Ignorance of the elliptical nature of some passive phrases often means that, when learners hear native speakers use *ser* and *estar* in such expressions, they believe that the native is using them indiscriminately. This is not the case. Native speakers may not always be able to tell you exactly why they have used one or other of the constructions, or give you a grammatical breakdown of *ser* and *estar* in this context, but **they** know what they mean and which verb to use to express this meaning.

Similarly, English speakers cannot always explain why they have used one linguistic structure rather than another. Relatively few people analyse their own language in this manner. They just use it instinctively.

An example of this is how, as a student, I found myself to be ignorant of exactly why, in English, on some occasions we use the word "any" and on others the word "some" in phrases such as "Is there *any* milk in the fridge?' and "Is there *some* milk in the fridge". It was not until a foreign student asked me to explain this

that I was forced to think about it (and look it up). The difference
—as anyone involved in the teaching of English as a foreign
language will know—is that 'some' is usually used when we are
expecting an affirmative answer, but we are checking to make
sure; while 'any' is used when we have no idea what the answer
might be. However, though many native English speakers may be
unaware of this rationale, they would instinctively know which of
these expressions to use in a particular circumstance. The same is
true of *ser* and *estar* for the native Spanish speaker.

Judging from the mistakes that one continually encounters among
learners, it seems that most are totally unaware of the possible
elliptical nature of the passive in Spanish. Not surprisingly,
therefore, students remain perplexed when they hear native
Spanish speakers say, for example when referring to a film
(*película*):

¿Dónde es la película?

They believe (wrongly) that the speaker is either making a
grammatical error by using the wrong verb, or that in such cases
ser and *estar* are interchangeable. Neither of these is the case. In
fact, the speaker is employing the passive voice here, and what is
being said in the above phrase is:

¿Dónde es [proyectada] la película?
(¿Where is the film being shown?)

This is an expression which one might hear in the context of an
enquiry about a specific room or hall in which something is taking
place. For instance: 'In which room/on which floor of this building
is the film being shown, the discussion being held?' etc.

On the other hand, had the speaker said:

¿Dónde está la película?

82

what would be understood here is 'Where is the roll/reel of film?'
—where is this object located?

In Spanish, as we said at the outset, depending on what one
wanted to say or emphasize a different 'to be' verb would be used
so as to eliminate the ambiguity that can be produced by one
all-purpose verb. As will be clear from the above phrases concern-
ing *la película* (the film), in English the ambiguity is removed by
the insertion of the words "being shown" which makes it clear that
we are referring to where something is taking place, rather than
to the location of an object, i.e., the roll or reel of film.

A hint for those students who feel confused as to when a question
should be posed as:

¿Dónde es...?

or

¿Dónde está...?

is to ask yourself if in English the words 'being given/shown', or
'taking place', etc. can be added to the end of your question. If
they can, then the question should be formulated with *ser*, e.g.,
'where is the meeting [taking place]?' (*¿dónde es la reunión?*);
'where is the talk [being given]?' (*¿dónde es la conferencia?*); 'where
is the concert [taking place]?' (*¿dónde es el concierto?*).

BUT:

In a question such as 'where is the cinema?' the words 'being
given', 'taking place', etc. , cannot be added and hence *estar* should
be used; 'where is the cinema?' (*¿dónde está el cine?*); 'where are my
notes?' (*¿dónde están mis apuntes?*); 'where is the car?' (*¿dónde está
el coche?*).

2) *Estar* with Past Participles

Estar is used with the past participle to describe a state which is the result of an action.

*La puerta **está** abierta**
(The door is open)

*El trabajo **está** terminado*
(The work is finished)

*María **está** sentada*
(Maria is seated)

In this construction (*estar* + past participle), the participle acts as an adjective, but this adjective does not qualify any inherent attribute or quality. It indicates Howness by denoting the state someone or something is in.

We saw earlier that when used with *ser*, the past participle can be omitted and still remain implicit in the phrase, and the same is true when it is used with *estar*. We often encounter phrases such as:

*Los ejercicios **están** bien*
*Los ejercicios **están** bien [hechos, escritos, etc.]*
(The exercises are well done, written, etc.)

*El proyecto **está** muy mal*
*El proyecto **está** muy mal [hecho,etc.]*
(The project is very badly done, etc.)

---

* abierta: irregular past participle of the verb *abrir* (to open)

We saw earlier that *ser* is used with an infinitive in generalizations (e.g., *fumar es malo.*) However, you will often hear *estar* used with infinitives in statements such as :

*[El] fumar en clase **está** muy mal*

This statement does not refer to smoking in general, but confines itself to the particular case of smoking in class. Furthermore, the phrase is another example of an ellipsis where the past participle is omitted:

*[El fumar en clase **está** muy mal [visto, etc.]*
(Smoking in class is frowned upon)
(lit. Smoking in class is badly seen)

Finally, we also saw that, when referring to origin or the material something is made of, *ser de* should be used (e.g., *es de oro*). Nevertheless, you will often encounter expressions such as:

Está *hecho de oro*
(It is made out of gold)

Está *tallado en madera*
(It is carved in wood)

Here *estar* indicates HOW something is made—it is the result of having employed or worked with certain materials. *Hecho* (made) and *tallado* (carved) are both past participles and, as mentioned above, the construction *estar* + past participle emphasizes the resulting state brought about by an action—in this case, the action of having carved or engraved.

Ser and *Estar* with Prices

This is another case where the difference in the use of *ser* and *estar* is slight. The distinction is mainly that of emphasis or context. When *ser* is used with prices it is almost as though the article or articles purchased had a fixed price which did not vary from day to day. Whereas when *estar* is used, the emphasis is on the circumstantial or fluctuating nature of the price: how much they stand at today; how much they are 'going for' today, etc.

In the context of your regular shopping, for example, if every Saturday you pop into your local greengrocer's to buy fruit, pears for example, you would probably say:

*¿A cuánto **están** las peras [hoy]?*

This could indicate that you already have a good idea of the approximate price, but you are enquiring about their price today —how the pears **stand** price-wise at the moment.

However, in the context of, say, visiting a large department store or an exclusive boutique, and enquiring about the price of a dress (*un vestido*) or a bottle of perfume (*un perfume*), you would NOT say: *¿A cuánto está este vestido?* or *¿A cuánto está este perfume?* In places like department stores you expect prices to be fixed , so there would be no day to day variation. Thus you would probably say:

*¿Cuánto **es** este vestido?*
¿Cuánto cuesta este vestido?
(What is the price of/ How much is this dress?)

*¿Cuánto **es** este perfume?*
(What is the price of/ How much is this perfume?)

The use of *ser* here denoted the fixed nature of the price.

Another expression often encountered is *¿A cómo son...?* for example: *¿A cómo son las fresas?* (How much are the strawberries?). On hearing this learners sometimes become confused between this expression and our first example, *¿A cuánto están las peras?* But, once again, *¿A cómo son.. ?* is just an elliptical, or shortened , form of the passive:

¿A cómo son las fresas?
(How much are the strawberries?)
¿A cómo son [vendidas] las fresas?
(How much are the strawberries being sold for?)

PRICES

SER	ESTAR
An elliptical (shortened) form of the passive voice.	The emphasis is on HOW the price **stands** at a specific time.
A)	
¿A cómo son las peras?	*¿A cuánto están las peras?*
¿A cómo son [vendidas] las peras?	*¿A cuánto están las peras [hoy]?*
(How much are the pears?)	(How much are the pears today?)
(What is the price of ...?	
Las peras son a ... el kilo.	*Las peras están a ... el kilo.*
(The pears are ... a kilo)	(The pears are ... a kilo)
B)	
¿Cuánto es [todo]?	
(What is the total?)	
(How much does it all come to?)	
¿Cuánto es el sofá?	
(How much is the sofa?)	
(What is the price of the sofa?)	

Estar with the Present Participle/Gerund:

In English, as we saw earlier, the present participle or gerund is formed by adding "ing" to a verb, e.g. smoking, walking, talking, etc.

In Spanish the gerund is formed by adding:

- *ando* to the stem of -*ar* verbs:

- *iendo* to the stem of -*er* and -*ir* verbs.

For example:

Andar (to walk)	—	*andando* (walking)
Beber (to drink)	—	*bebiendo* (drinking)
Vivir (to live)	—	*viviendo* (living)

As in English, the gerund is used to form the continuous or progressive tenses, in the formula: **estar + gerund.** These tenses inform us of the STATE someone/something is in—HOW they are engaged or situated. They indicate an action or situation taking place at the particular time we have in mind. This can be in the past, present or future. However, the emphasis is always on the unfinished or temporary nature of the situation or action during that period of time.

Los trabajadores **están** *trabajando* — The workers are working
Los alumnos **están** *estudiando ahora* — The students are studying
at the moment

The only difference between the continuous tenses in English and Spanish is that they are employed much less frequently in Spanish —their use generally being reserved for emphasizing the state or duration. This is so because the simple tenses in Spanish can also convey the often less emphatic meaning of the English continuous tenses. That is to say, depending on the context, the phrase _Pedro come_ can be translated as either "Pedro eats" (referring to what Pedro usually does) and "Pedro is eating" (referring to what Pedro is doing at the moment).

However, if we encounter:

Pedro **está** comiendo

the very use of _estar_ immediately indicates that greater stress is being placed on the duration of the state Pedro is in—the state of eating.

* * *

CHAPTER FOUR

Intentions and Words

IV

1. CHALLENGING THE EXCEPTIONS

We have already seen how many of the so-called 'exceptions' regarding the use of *ser* and *estar* with certain words are covered and explained by the application of the principle of Whatness and Howness. We have also seen that in any analysis of the use of *ser* or *estar*, one or more of thrce factors should be taken into account:

1)   In many cases it is a question of choice as to which of the two verbs is used and , as mentioned earlier, this will depend on your intended meaning. Remember those cases already analysed, such as:

> *Juan **es** muy inteligente*
> *Juan **está** muy inteligente*
>
> *El Papa **es** muy católico*
> *El Papa no **está** muy católico*

2)   There are many cases (particularly in colloquial speech) which are clearly elliptical—words (like the past participle etc.) may be omitted, and awareness of this is necessary in order to know which verb to use. For example:

> *La clase **es** en el quinto piso*
> *La clase **está** en el quinto piso*
>
> *Fumar **es** malo*
> *Fumar en clase **está** mal*

3)   Even when words or phrases are used figuratively or metaphorically, they are still subject to the principle of Whatness and Howness:

Estar en la luna
Ser una perdida

In this section we shall analyse some of those words which when used with *ser* and *estar* take on different meanings. In doing this you will see how it is the very principle of Whatness and Howness itself which serves to illuminate these different meanings.

We shall then go on to look at some of those words which, it has often been suggested, should only be used with one of the 'to be' verbs. This in fact is not totally accurate—as we glimpsed earlier, in chapter two, when referring to the nature of certain qualities denoted by *ser* and *estar*. The application of the principle of Whatness and Howness in this context will demonstrate how these words can be used very effectively with the other 'to be' verb.

*   *   *

Same Word—Different Meaning

There are many adjectives and past participles functioning as adjectives which, when used with *ser* and *estar*, undergo a change of meaning. Nevertheless, these are still governed by the same principle. When *ser* is employed with these words you will see that what is being indicated or denoted is WHAT sort of a person or thing someone/something is. While if used with *estar* the meaning will once again be one of HOWNESS as the verb will specifically refer to the state the person/thing is in.

94

In this way, the meaning of the word may vary, but the principle remains firm and reliable—furthermore, it sheds light on the different meaning of the words in question. Examples of the most common words in this category are given below.

A) *Ser* and *Estar* with the Past Participle used as an Adjective:

Ser = WHATNESS	*Estar* = HOWNESS
What someone/ something is	How someone/something is

abierto/a (frank)
El es muy abierto
El es [un hombre] muy abierto
(He is very frank)

abierto/a (open)
El está abierto a toda crítica

(He is open to all criticism)

aburrido/a (boring)
Es muy aburrida
Es [una persona*] muy aburrida
(She is a very boring person)

aburrido/a (bored)
Está muy aburrida

(She is very bored)

callado/a (taciturn/quiet)
La niña es tan callada
(She is such a quiet girl)
(lit. The girl is so taciturn)

callado/a (silent/ quiet)
La niña está tan callada
(The girl is so quiet [at the moment]

---

* And so on with other examples under *ser* - the words *persona*, *hombre, mujer, cosa,* will not be repeated in the other cases cited.

despierto/a
(alert/sharp/clever)
El chico es muy despierto
(The boy is very clever)

despierto/a (awake)
El chico aún no está despierto
(The boy is not awake yet)

decidido/a (resolute)
María es muy decidida
(Maria is a very resolute wo-
man)

decidido/a (resolved/ decided)
Ella aún no está decidida
(She is still undecided)

divertido/a (amusing)
El profesor es tan divertido
(The teacher is so amusing)

divertido/a (amused)
El alumno no está divertido
(The pupil is not amused)

La película es divertida
(The film is funny/amusing)

interesado/a (selfish)
Es [un hombre] tan interesado
(He is such a selfish man)

interesado/a (interested)
Sí, estoy interesado
(Yes, I am interested)

B) *Ser* and *Estar* used with Adjectives:

atento/a (courteous/considerate)
María es muy atenta
(María is very courteous)

atento/a (attentive)
El está atento en clase
(He is attentive in class)

NOTE:

And in numerous other cases, *atento/a* can also be used with **estar** to indicate behaviour/appearance,etc. at a specific time:

María está muy atenta hoy
(María is very courteous to-day)

bueno/a (good by nature)
See pages 40 and 56.

bueno/a (tasty/ 'hot dish')
See pages 40 and 56.

débil (weak by nature)
Antonio es débil
(Antonio is weak - this can refer to both character and physical strength)

débil (weak/feeble health-wise)
Antonio está débil
(Antonio is [feeling] weak)

listo/a (clever)
Mi hijo es muy listo
(My son is very clever)

listo/a (ready)
Mi hijo todavía no está listo
(My son is not ready yet)

loco/a (insane)
Tu propuesta es loca
(Your proposal is insane)

loco/a (crazy, mad)
Ana está loca
(Ana is mad—referring to her behaviour)

NOTE:

Ser [un/una] loco/a =
To be an insane person, or a daring person

negro/a (black)
El carbón es negro
(Coal is black)

negro/a (furious)
Mi padre está negro conmigo
(My father is furious with me)

nuevo/a (brand new)
El coche es nuevo
(The car is new)

nuevo/a (in good condition)
El coche está nuevo
(The car is in good condition)

orgulloso/a (arrogant/conceited)
Ese actor es muy orgulloso
(That actor is very conceited)

orgulloso/a (proud)
El está orgulloso de su hijo
(He is very proud of his son)

rico/a (rich/wealthy)
Mis amigos son muy ricos
(My friends are very rich)

rico/a (delicious)
El pescado está rico
(The fish is delicious)

seguro/a (safe/reliable)
Este coche es muy seguro
(This car is very reliable)

seguro/a (sure/positive)
No estoy seguro de eso
(I am not sure about that)

NOTE:

Estar seguro de sí mismo =
To be self-confident. *Estar* is used here as it refers to HOW the person feels.

torpe (dim-witted)
Este alumno es muy torpe
(This student is very dim)

torpe (clumsy)
Estás torpe
(You are clumsy)

verde (green)
El abrigo es verde
(The coat is green)

verde (immature/unripe)
Las peras están verdes
(The pears are unripe)

NOTE:

verde can also mean:
        dirty/smutty/blue
Es una película verde
(It's a blue film)

Es un chiste verde
(It's a dirty /blue/smutty joke)

Es un viejo verde
(He is a dirty old man)

violento/a (violent or
                      embarrassing)
Ese hombre es muy violento
(That man is very violent)

La situación es violenta
(The situation is
                  embarrassing)

vivo/a (lively/vivid)
Es [una niña] muy viva
(She is very lively)

La descripción es tan viva
(The description is so vivid)

NOTE:

Ser un vivo = To be sly, crafty
Eres un vivo y un carota
(You are crafty and cheeky)

Ser muerto/a = To be killed

This is another example of the passive voice where *ser* is used with the past participle (*muerto/a*):

violento/a (embarrassed)
Están violentos
(They are/feel embarrassed)

vivo/a (alive)
Estoy vivo
(I am alive)

NOTE:

Estar muerto/a = To be dead/lifeless
The opposite of *estar vivo* is *estar muerto.*
(*Estar muerto* can be either a temporary or permanent state of being depending on one's religious beliefs.)

[El] Fue muerto en un accidente
(He was killed in an accident)

El perro está muerto
(The dog is dead/lifeless)
The expression *estar muerto/a*
(just as its equivalent in English) can have a figurative meaning:

Estoy más muerto que vivo
(I'm more dead than alive)

Estoy muerto de cansancio
(I'm dead tired)

Ser un muerto = To be a corpse
¿Qué es eso? Es un muerto
(What is that ? It is a corpse)

* * *

One still comes across grammars which set out one list of words to be used only with *ser*, and another which should only be used with *estar*.

Some of the words which most frequently feature on the *ser* list are:

    feliz (happy), *pobre* (poor), *culpable* (guilty), *inocente* (innocent), *desgraciado/a* (unfortunate/wretched), *cabezota* (bigheaded), *perezoso/a* (lazy), *estúpido/a* (stupid), *imbécil* (imbecil), *inteligente* (intelligent), *trabajador/a* (hardworking), *gruñón/a* (grumpy/grumbling), etc.

While some of those often encountered on the *estar* list are:

> *contento/a* (content/happy), *harto/a* (fed-up), *despistado/a* (absent-minded), *borracho/a* (drunk), *emocionado/a* (deeply moved/touched), *desilusionado/a* (disillusioned/disappointed), *deprimido/a* (depressed), *furioso/a* (furious), *dispuesto/a* (ready/prepared), *preocupado/a* (worried), *disgustado/a* (annoyed/ displeased), *nervioso/a* (nervous), etc.

Yet, as we indicated earlier, (in Chapter Two) when dealing with adjectives like *inteligente, cariñoso/a, guapo/a,* etc., many of these words can also be used with the other 'to be' verb so as to convey a different meaning or nuance. This is also true of many of the words on the above lists, particularly those on the *ser* list.

First we will look at just a couple of words from the *ser* list as a reminder of how the shade of meaning or emphasis changes when used with *estar*.

Taking *feliz* and *perezoso/a*, it is true that when describing someone *ser* is usually used with these words to indicate the sort of person he/she is—someone of a naturally happy or lazy disposition. Yet all of us, even those of miserable disposition, can have days when things are going particularly well or the news is especially good and consequently we could say quite legitimately:

> **Estoy** *muy feliz hoy*
> (I'm very happy today)

Likewise even the most active people are allowed to have off days and say:

> **Estoy** *perezoso/a hoy*
> (I'm [feeling] lazy today)

In the case of words on the *estar* list, it is true that, when these are employed as adjectives, they are used in conjunction with *estar*. However, you may often encounter expressions such as:

*Juan **está** nervioso*
(Juan is nervous)
(Juan is in a nervous state)

and :

*Juan **es** nervioso*
(Juan is a nervous person)

As explained in Chapter Two, this is so because the second case, *Juan **es** nervioso*, is an elliptical form of *Juan es [un hombre de temperamento] nervioso* (Juan is a man of nervous temperament) and here the emphasis is on Whatness.

Similarly with other words like *borracho/a* or *despistado/a* which, when used with *estar*, are adjectives emphasizing the state someone is in:

Está *borracho* — He is drunk
Está *despistado* — He is absent minded
(He is in an absent-minded state)

but when used with *ser*, become nouns denoting what someone is:

Es *un borracho* — He is a drunkard
Es *un despistado* — He is an absent-minded sort of person

SIGNPOSTS

The signposts you should follow to help you pick your way
through the *ser* and *estar* minefield are:

TO BE NICE

a) To Refer to Natural Attributes,
   To Be Openly Complimentary: **USE *SER* WITH
                                    POSITIVE QUALITIES**

Es inteligente	— He/she is intelligent
Es guapo/a	— He/she is beautiful

b) To Refer to Temporary State,
   Not to Offend: **USE *ESTAR* WITH
                      NEGATIVE QUALITIES**

Está torpe (hoy) —	He/she is dim (today)
Está tonto/a (hoy) —	He/she is silly (today)

TO BE NASTY

a) To Refer to Natural Attributes,
   To Be Insulting: **USE *SER* WITH
                        NEGATIVE QUALITIES**

Es estúpido/a	— He/she is stupid
Es feo/a	— He/she is ugly

b) To Refer to Temporary State,
   **To Be Sarcastic or
   Give Back-Handed Compliment:** **USE *ESTAR* WITH
                                  POSITIVE QUALITIES**

*¡Qué listo **estás** hoy!*	— How clever you are today!
***Estás** muy comprensivo*	— You are very understanding [at the moment]

SOME IDIOMATIC EXPRESSIONS
WITH *SER* AND *ESTAR*

1. With *Estar*—Howness

ESTAR:	**TO BE:**
ajeno de:	ignorant/ unaware of
en el ajo:	in the know
más alegre que unas Pascuas:	as happy as a sandboy/a lark
a la altura de:	to be up to/equal to [the task/the occasion]
a sus anchas:	to feel at ease/home
metido en años:	getting on in years
a la antigua:	in the old fashioned way
sobre ascuas:	on pins and needles/on tenter hooks
en boga:	in fashion
calado/mojado hasta los huesos:	soaked/drenched/wet through
más callado que en misa:	as quiet as a mouse

ESTAR: ## TO BE:

más claro que el agua: as plain as a pike staff/
                                                   the nose on one's face:
                                                   crystal clear

más contento que unas   as happy as a sandboy/a
Pascuas: lark

al corriente de: up to date on

a las duras y a las   take the rough with the
maduras: smooth

con la escopeta cargada: to be ready to pounce on

entre la espada y la
pared: between the devil and
                                                  the deep blue sea
en la flor de la vida:
                                                  in the prime of life
en la gloria:
                                                  in one's element
de guardia:
                                                  on duty/on stand-by
en guardia:
                                                  on one's guard
más a gusto que un
guarro en una charca: as snug as a bug in a rug

en los huesos:
                                                  nothing but skin and
                                                  bone
pendiente de un hilo:
                                                  hanging by a thread
bajo llave:
                                                  under lock and key
loco de remate:
                                                  raving mad

ESTAR: TO BE:

de más: in the way; superfluous

la pelota en el tejado: nothing has been decided yet

a las puertas de la muerte: at death's door

más sano que una pera: as fit as a fiddle/ as sound as a bell

al sol que más calienta: to know which side one's bread is buttered on

en un tris de: on the point of; within an inch of

hecho un tronco: to be sound asleep

en las últimas: on one's last legs

2) With *Ser*—Whatness

SER: TO BE:

muy de adentro: like one of the family

el blanco de: the centre of

más bruto que un arado: as thick as two short planks

de cal y canto: tough, strong

otro cantar: a different kettle of fish; another story

SER:	TO BE:
un cero a la izquierda:	a nobody; useless
algo corriente y moliente:	run-of- the-mill
el colmo:	the limit
coser y cantar:	a piece of cake: child's play
un cuento de hadas:	a fairy tale
un cuento chino:	a cock-and-bull story
más delgado que una caña/ palo:	as thin as a rake
diferente como de la noche al día:	as different as chalk and cheese
más fresco que una lechuga:	as cool as a cucumber
harina de otro costal:	a different kettle of fish/another story/ a horse of a different colour
un hueso duro de roer:	a tough nut to crack
un hombre de/con pelo en pecho:	a real he-man
iguales como dos gotas de agua:	as like as two peas

SER:

Jauja*
Eso es Jauja:

TO BE:

the Promised Land
that's the Promised Land,
the land of milk and
honey

nada del otro jueves:
no es nada del otro
jueves:

nothing special
it's nothing special/
nothing out of the
ordinary

más limpio que una
patena:

as clean as a new pin

liso como una tabla:

as flat as a pancake

la manzana de la
discordia:

the bone of contention

el ojo derecho de:

the favourite/darling of

pan comido:

a piece of cake/as easy as
pie

peor el remedio que la
enfermedad:

the cure [is] worse than
the disease

más sordo que una tapia:

as deaf as a post

más tieso que un palo
seco/una mojama:

as stiff as a poker

un trabalenguas:

a tongue twister

tortas y pan pintado:

a piece of cake/ as easy as
falling off a log

uña y carne:

as thick as thieves/hand
in glove

*¿Estamos aquí o en Jauja?: Where do you think you are?

SOME 'COLOURFUL' EXPRESSIONS
WITH *SER* AND *ESTAR*

ESTAR: **TO BE**

amoratado/a: purple; blue (with cold); livid

en blanco: blank
(El libro de los gustos   (There's no accounting for
está en blanco):   taste)

lila: lilac; foolish, silly

negro con alguien: angry/furious with someone
con la negra: to have bad luck
(tener la negra)

rojo como un tomate: red as a beetroot
rojo de furia/ira: red with anger/rage
al rojo vivo: red hot

SER   **TO BE**

blanco/a :   white
el blanco de: to be the centre of
un cheque en blanco: a blank cheque

rojo/a: red
un rojo: red (politically), communist

rosa: pink
una película muy rosa: a sentimental film

verde: green
                                unripe, immature
una película verde: a blue film

un viejo verde: a dirty old man

109

SER AND *ESTAR* IN THE ANIMAL KINGDOM

AGUILA
Ser un águila:

an eagle;
fig: quick-witted, extremely clever, wily bird

ARAÑA
Ser una araña:

a spider;
fig: resourceful/calculating person; a prostitute

ARDILLA
Ser una ardilla:

a squirrel
fig: an agile/active person, a go-getter

ASNO
Ser un asno:

an ass, donkey;
fig: idiot, dolt

ATUN
Ser un atún:
Ser un pedazo de atún:

a tuna fish
to be stupid, a dim-wit

BALLENA
Ser una ballena:

a whale;
to be as fat as a cow

BURRO/A
Ser un burro:

a donkey;
fig: stupid, dolt ; obstinate

CABRA
Ser una cabra:
una cabra loca:

a female goat
to be mad, wild

Estar (como una) cabra:

to be crazy/to be as mad as a hatter/ a March hare

CERDO/A
Ser un cerdo:

a pig; fig: dirty

Estar hecho un cerdo:

to be dirty; behave in a slovenly manner

110

CORDERITO
Ser un corderito:

a baby lamb:
a meek and mild person

COCHINO/A
Ser un cochino:

a pig (see *cerdo*)

CONEJO/A
Ser un conejo:
una coneja:

a rabbit
a doe rabbit;
fig: to be fertile

CONEJILLO
Ser un conejillo
de Indias:

a guinea pig

GALLINA
Ser una gallina:

a hen;
fig: coward, a yellow-belly

Estar como una gallina
en corral ajeno:

to be like a fish out of water

GALLITO
Ser un gallito:

a small cock;
fig: a show-off; cock of the
walk

Ser el gallito del grupo:

to be a cock of the walk, top
dog

GALLO
Ser un gallo:

lit: a cock;
fig: a bully

Ser un gallo de pelea:

a fighting cock

GANSO/A
Ser un ganso:

a goose;
fig: a sloppy, dim foolish, person

Estar ganso:
Estar hecho un ganso:

to be idle , sloppy, indolent
to behave like an idler

HORMIGA
Ser una hormiga:

lit. an ant;
fig: thrifty, hardworking

111

LAGARTA
Ser una lagarta:

a female lizard;
fig: an astute, sly woman; a bitch

LAGARTIJA
Ser una lagartija:
Ser un rabo de lagartija:

a small lizard;
fig; somone full of nervous energy

LINCE
Ser un lince:

a lynx;
fig: sharp-eyed, shrewd

LORO
Ser un loro:

a parrot;
fig: a chatterbox, an ugly woman

MULO/A
Ser un mulo:

a mule;
fig: stubborn; thick

Ser terco como una mula:

to be as stubborn as a mule

OVEJA
Ser una oveja:

lit: a sheep

Ser la oveja negra de la familia:

to be the black sheep of the family

PAJARO/A
Ser un pájaro:

a bird;
fig: a sly/crafty person

Ser un pájaro de cuenta:

to be a big shot, bigwig

PAJARRACO/A
Ser un pajarraco:

a big ugly bird;
fig: an astute and malignant person

PAJARITO
Ser un pajarito:

a baby bird;
fig: a small, skinny person

PAPAGAYO

Ser un papagayo:	a parrot; fig: chatterbox

PATO

Ser un pato:	a duck; fig: a bore/ dull person

PAVO/A

Ser un pavo:	a turkey; fig: to be a silly, dull, ingenuous person
No seas un pavo:	Don't be silly
Estar pavo:	to be dull, silly (HOWNESS)
Estar en la edad del pavo:	to be at the awkward age of an adolescent

PERRA

Ser una perra:	a female dog, a bitch
una perra gorda:	lit. a fat female dog; fig; a 10-*céntimo* coin
una perra chica:	fig: a 5-*céntimo* coin

PEZ

Ser un pez:	a fish
un pez gordo:	to be a bigshot, a bigwig
Estar pez:	to be hopeless at/to know absolutely nothing about
Estar como el pez en el agua:	to feel at ease/at home

POLLO

Ser un pollo:	a chicken; fig: young man (NOTE: not a coward; see *gallina*)

POLLITO/A

Ser un pollito:	a baby chicken; fig: a chick; a youngster

RATA

Ser una rata:	a rat; fig: a mean person
Ser más pobre que una rata:	to be as poor as a church mouse (WHATNESS)
Estar más pobre que una rata:	to be as poor as a church mouse (HOWNESS)

RATON

Ser un ratón:	a mouse
Ser un ratón de biblioteca:	to be a bookworm

RENACUAJO

Ser un renacuajo:	a tadpole; small and/or insignificant person, a little runt, fig: shrimp

TOPO

Ser un topo:	a mole
Ser más ciego que un topo:	to be as blind as a bat

TORO

Ser un toro:	a bull; a solidly-built man, tough guy, he-man

TORTUGA

Ser una tortuga:	a tortoise, a turtle; fig: a slow person

VACA

Ser una vaca:	a cow; fig: a very fat woman

VIBORA

Ser una víbora:	a viper: fig: malignant person

ZORRO/A

Ser un zorro:	a fox; fig: astute, sly
Ser una zorra:	a vixen; fig; astute, sly; a prostitute

STATES OF BEING

The expressions listed under the sub-headings below have a common denominator in their use of the verb *estar* to denote a particular state of being. The English translations are intended to provide only the general meaning—as many of these expressions are used synonymously. The list is not meant to be exhaustive.

Anger: To be angry:

Estar	disgustado/a enfadado/a picado/a	to be angry, annoyed, cross
	cabreado/a rabiando (con rabia) volado/a enojado/a encolerizado/a	to be angry, raging, fuming, foaming
	con malas pulgas (tener malas pulgas) de malas de mala leche	to be angry, nasty, vindictive, bad-tempered
	endemoniado/a dado al diablo	to be possessed of the devil, furious, raging
	emberrenchinado/a	to fly into a rage/a tantrum
	hasta la coronilla hasta los cojones hasta las tetas	to be fed up to the back teeth, annoyed, angry

	por las nubes	to be angry, furious, wild
	subido a la parra	with rage, to go up the wall
	que trina	
	que trepa por las paredes	
	hecho un basilisco	to be very angry, enraged

Astonishment: To be astonished:

Estar	asombrado/a	to be astonished, amazed
	admirado/a	
	maravillado/a	
	atónito/a	to be flabbergasted, stunned,
	estupefacto/a	thunder-struck,dumb-founded
	pasmado/a	
	suspendido/a	
	alucinado/a	as above; also: deluded

Drunkenness: To be drunk:

Estar	borracho/a	to be drunk
	bebido/a	
	embriagado/a	
	beodo/a	
	ebrio/a	
	trompa	to be drunk, sozzled, tight
	mamado/a	
	ahumado/a	
	ajumado/a	
	tajado/a	

piripi	to be tipsy, tight
con una melopea (tener una melopea) con una merluza (tener una merluza) con una mona (tener una mona) hecho un trapo hecho una cuba hecho una uva	to be blind drunk, as drunk as a lord, as drunk as a fiddler
de resaca	to have a hangover
entre dos luces entre Pinto y Valdemoro	to be half-drunk, tipsy

NOTE: *Ser* [un] borracho: to be a drunkard

Fear: To be afraid:

Estar miedoso/a (con miedo) temeroso/a asustado/a	to be afraid, alarmed, scared
acobardado/a acoquinado/a acochinado/a temblando	to be frightened, scared, feel intimidated

aterrorizado/a	to be afraid, pertrified, frightened to death, terrified
cagado/a	
acojonado/a	
muerto/a de miedo	
(caerse muerto/a de	
miedo)	
más muerto que vivo	
patitieso/a	
yerto/a	
(quedarse yerto/a)	
con el alma en un hilo	to be afraid, frightened out of one's wits
con un nudo en la garganta	
(atravesarse un nudo en la garganta)	
con los pelos de punta	to make one's hair stand on end
(ponerse los pelos de punta)	

NOTE: *Ser* un miedoso: to be a timorous person
          un cagón: to be a coward, a chicken

Madness: To be mad:

Estar	loco/a	
	majareta	to be mad, crazy, barmy,
	chiflado/a	insane, off one's head
	chaveta	
	mochales	
	desequilibrado/a	to be unbalanced
	cruzado/a	to be mad, cracked, unhing-
	desconectado/a	ed, crazy, round the bend
	desvariado/a	
	disparatado/a	
	ido/a	
	pirado/a	
	tocado/a de la cabeza	to be touched (in the head),
	tocado/a del ala	crazy
	fuera de su acuerdo	to be mad, deranged, out of
	fuera de juicio	one's -mind-wits - senses
	falto de juicio	
	como una chota	to be as mad as a hatter,
	como un cencerro	stark staring mad, off one's
	[como una] cabra	head, out of one's mind
	loco de remate	raving mad

> NOTE: *Ser* [un/una]
> loco de atar: to be a mad person

Nakedness: To be naked:

Estar	desnudo/a desplumado/a pelado/a	to be naked, undressed, un- clothed, in one's birthday suit
	al natural a culo de pájaro	to be naked, in the buff
	en pelota(s) en cueros/en cueros vivos en cuerpo de camisa	to be stark naked
	in puribus	in puris naturalibus

Pregnancy: To be pregnant:

Estar	embarazada preñada grávida (poetic) encinta en estado en los meses mayores	to be pregnant, expecting (a baby)
	fuera de cuenta	expecting to give birth any day now
	dando a luz de parto pariendo	to be in labour, giving birth
NOTE:	*Ser* una primeriza	— a woman bearing her first child
	una cadañera	— a woman who gives birth annually
	una coneja	— a rabbit

Sexual Excitement: To be sexually aroused:

Estar	cachondo/a caliente calentón/na con ganas salido/a	to be excited, to feel sexy, hot, horny
	bueno/a (más bueno/a que...)	to be hot, sexy
	como un tren cojonudo/a	to be dishy, red-hot
	de marcha de juerga	to be excited, feel sexy; also: to live it up, to have a good time
	hecho un don Juan	to act like a real Don Juan

NOTE:	*Ser* un don Juan: un viejo verde:	to be a Don Juan to be a dirty old man

2. DIGGING UP THE ROOTS

In chapter one we saw that *ser* and *estar* are derived from Latin.

Ser (from *esse*) denotes the essence or particular nature of a thing —that which makes it what it is. Words, in both English and Spanish, which derive from this source are relatively few. Words such as *esencia*, (essence), *esencial* (essential), *ente* (entity/being), *entidad* (entity) are examples of the most common ones. The same is true for the corresponding Greek root *on, ontos* (being), which gives us such technical words as *ontología* (ontology), *ontológico* (ontological), *ontólogo* (ontologist), *ontogénesis* (ontogenesis), *ontogenia* (ontogeny).

Estar is from the Latin *stare* (to stand), but this in turn has been traced to an ancient Indo-European root *sta*. *Sta* implies stability —the state or attribute of being able to stand firm, of being stable or not easily moved.

In contrast to *esse*, the *sta* root is found in numerous words in both Spanish and English. It generally indicates how or where someone or something stands—the particular location, position, condition, situation, manner, etc. Thus the word status, for example, refers to a person's standing, i.e. his/her rank, social or economic position, etc. A stable is a standing or lodging place for horses. A stadium is a place where people (spectators) stand. A stage is a place where actors stand. Stance refers to the way a person stands —posture, manner,etc. A statute is a legislative enactment, a firm rule or law.

The list below gives some of the most common words in Spanish which contain the *sta* root and which have an almost identical or near equivalent English spelling. In many cases the difference is simply that in Spanish (a vocalic language) the word starts with the vowel 'e', while in English (a more consonantal language) it begins directly with the 's' of the *sta* root. Other differences in orthography are those of the common equivalent endings, such as *-dad* and *-mente* in Spanish, which often correspond to -ty and -ly respectively in English. For example *estabilidad* (stability), *constantemente* (constantly).

This list is not meant to be exhaustive, nor does it include any of the words in either language which contain the *sta* root but which do not have a similar spelling in the other. Examples of such words in English which have a completely different Spanish equivalent are: stall (*puesto*), stale (*añejo*), staff (*vara/bastón*), staple (*producto* or *artículo principal*). While examples of such words in Spanish are: *estante* (shelf), *bienestar* (well-being), *malestar* (discomfort).

Some Common Words Containing The *STA* Root

estabilidad	stability
estabilizador	stabilizer
estabilizar	to stabilize
estable	stable (steady, firmly fixed, settled)
inestabilidad	instability
inestable	unstable
establecer	to establish
establecimiento	establishment
restablecer	reestablish
restablecimiento	reestablishment
establero	stableboy
establo	stable (standing/ dwelling place for horses, cows, etc.)

estabular	to stable
estación	station
estacionamiento	stationing
estacionar	to station
estacionario	stationary
estadio	stadium
estadista	statesman or statistician
estadística	statistics
estado	state, status
estancamiento	stagnation
estancarse	to stagnate
estancia	stay or stanza
estandarte	standard
estatal	state (adj.)
estático	static
estatismo	statism
estatua	statue
estatuario	statuary
estatura	stature
estatutario	statutory
estatuto	statute
constancia	constancy
constante	constant
constatar	to state
inconstancia	inconstancy
inconstante	inconstant
contrastable	contrastable
contrastar	to contrast
contraste	contrast
distancia	distance
distante	distant
instante	instant
instantáneo	instantaneous
obstáculo	obstacle

PART II

MASTERING *SER* AND *ESTAR* AT LAST!

Part II

Part II offers a practical demonstration of the important role *ser* and *estar* play in the art of mastering Spanish. It is divided into four chapters:

Chapter 5: Joking and Playing Around with *Ser* and *Estar*

Chapter 6: *Ser* and *Estar* in Dialogue

Chapter 7: *Ser* and *Estar*—the Cornerstone of Creative Language

Chapter 8: A Text Analysis—*Juan el malas pulgas*

The first three chapters provide original material in which *ser* and *estar* are employed as the main vehicles of expressions. You will meet them for instance:

— in character sketches: for example in *Los tres Juanes, Pepe el churretoso*, etc. ;

— in dialogue: *ser* and *estar* in every-day, colloquial use and social encounters, as for example in *Dos abuelas a la antigua usanza*, and most of chapter 6;

— in humorous repartee—joking and playing around with *ser* and *estar*: as in the *diálogos de besugos* (playing on words and talking at cross purposes) found throughout chapter 5;

— in more poetic language: as in *Una tarde gris de bostezo*, etc.

You will see that *ser* and *estar* are at once the subject, the building blocks, and the main linguistic protagonists in all these illustrative texts.

Notes on vocabulary and idioms are provided at the end of those texts thought to contain linguistic difficulties, such as colloquialisms, figurative meanings, play on words, proverbs, etc.—particularly those relating to *ser* and *estar*.

As a further aid for those who would like a practical illustration of the use and implications of *ser* and *estar* in these texts, the character sketch *JUAN EL MALAS PULGAS* has been analysed in detail in chapter 8. This analysis is intended to serve as a guide to the way the other texts should be read and studied.

* * *

CHAPTER FIVE

Joking and Playing Around
with *Ser* and *Estar*

V

CONTENTS:

ESTAR DE MONOS

Yo: No es lo mismo estar mona que ser mona que ser una mona muy mona.

Tú: Claro que no. Como que todos sabemos que la mona vestida de seda, mona se queda. Que siempre es mona.

Yo: Pero hay monos que son muy monos, y otros que son más feos que Picio.

Tú: Pero en tu caso, anda que tú ... ¡Tú estás de un mono!

Yo: ¡Pues mira quién habla! Tú, ¡que eres el último mono!

Tú: ¡Vete a freír monas!

Yo: Y tú, ¡ a dormir la tuya!

Vocabulary and Idioms:

Ser un/una mono/a:	to be an ape, monkey; fig: a mimic, ugly monkey
Ser mono/a:	to be good-looking, pretty, nice
Estar mono/a:	to look nice, pretty
Estar de un mono:	to be a real joker, crazy, a nincompoop; to be well turned-out, good looking
Estar de monos:	to be at daggers drawn, to be at odds
Ser el último mono:	to be least important, a nobody
Ser más feo que Picio:	to be as ugly as sin
La mona, vestida de seda, mona se queda:	you can't make a silk purse out of a sow's ear
¡Vete a freír monas!:	Get lost! Go jump in a lake!
Dormir la mona:	to sleep it off (after drinking)

MOSCA:

UNA MOSCA PICAPICA

Yo: ¿Qué mosca te ha picado?

Tú: A mí ninguna, ¿Y a ti?

Yo: Pues estás mosqueado.

Tú: No estoy mosca.

Yo: Y si no estás mosca, ¿por qué te picas?

Tú: No me pico.

Yo: ¿Que no? Pues estás con un picor que... ¡Ni que estuvieras con urticaria! ¡Ni que fueras una mosca con el picapica!

Tú: ¡Y no eres tú pesado, ¿eh?! Ni estoy mosca, ni soy una mosca, ¿está claro?

Yo: Sí, ¡clarísimo!... Ahora va a resultar que sólo eres una mosquita muerta, ¿verdad?

Tú: ¡Y tú un moscón bien pesado!

Vocabulary and Idioms:

Una mosca:	a fly; fig: a pest, a bore
Ser una mosca:	fig: to be a pest, a bore
Un moscón:	lit: a bluebottle; fig: a pest, nuisance
Ser una mosquita muerta:	lit: to be a dead fly; fig: to look as if butter wouldn't melt in one's mouth, to be a hypocrite, a slyboots
Estar mosca/mosqueado: (Estar con una mosca en/detrás de la oreja)	to be distrustful, to smell a rat; to be angry (with someone), to be hot under the collar
¿Qué mosca te ha picado?	What's wrong with/bothering you?
¿Por qué te picas?:	Why are you so irritable? Why do you take offence (so easily)?
Picapica, (polvos de picapica)	itching powder; fig: irritating, irritated

DINERO (I)

SIN UNA RUBIA NI UNA BLANCA

Yo: ¿Me prestas dinero, que me he quedado sin un céntimo?

Tú: Lo siento, pero estoy pelado.

Yo: ¿Pelado tú con todo el pelo que tienes?

Tú: Te repito que estoy en pelotas. De veras, estoy sin blanca.

Yo: Ya lo creo. Tú estás sin una blanca y sin una rubia.

Tú: Pues aunque no lo creas, es verdad. Estoy sin una perra. No tengo ni una perra gorda en el bolsillo.

Yo: Claro, ¡cómo va a caber en tu bolsillo una perra gorda! Sobre todo si es tan gorda como tu perra. ¡Vaya perraza, y lo fiera que es! No, gracias. Quédate con tu perra.

Tú: Pues tómalo a broma, si quieres. Pero que conste que es cierto. Ni siquiera podría prestarte una perra chica.

Yo: Gracias, de nuevo, pero no te molestes. Yo no quiero ni una perra gorda, ni una perra chica. Sólo te pido un duro.

Tú: Eres duro de mollera, ¿eh? ¿No me crees?

Yo: Pues no. Porque tú eres rico. Como si yo no supiera que estás forrado, ¡pero bien forrado de billetes que estás tú!

Tú: Pues mira. ¿Ves? Mi cartera está vacía... Mis bolsillos están vacíos también. Seré todo lo rico que quieras, pero estoy pobre. Estoy tan pobre como tú.

Yo: ¡Cómo no! Ahora va a resultar que tú estás sin una blanca, sin una rubia, y sin ni siquiera calzoncillos, ¿no? Vamos, ¡que estás en pelotas, chico!

Vocabulary and Idioms:

Una rubia:	a blonde (woman); fam: a one-peseta coin of light golden colour
Una blanca:	fam: an old copper coin
Blanca:	woman's name
Estar sin blanca:	fam: to be broke
Estar pelado:	lit: to be hairless; fam: to be broke
Estar en pelotas:	fam: to be stark naked; to be broke
Una perra:	lit: female dog; fam: an old coin
Unas perras:	fam: a few coppers, small change
Una perra gorda:	fam: an old coin to value of 10 *céntimos*
Una perra chica:	fam: an old coin to value of 5 *céntimos*
Estar sin una perra:	fam: to be penniless, to be broke
Un duro:	fam: a five-peseta coin
Ser duro de mollera:	fam: to be dense, pigheaded
Estar forrado de (seda, etc.)	lit: to be lined (with silk)
Estar forrado de dinero:	fam: to be loaded with money

DINERO (II)

FORRADO EN CHATARRA

Yo: Ese ya no es de los nuestros. Desde que está metido en negocios de chatarra, está de un millonario que no le cabe el dinero encima. ¡Se está forrando!

Tú: ¡Como que está de un nuevo rico que da asco! Dicen que está nadando en dinero.

Yo: **Pues ¿sabes qué te digo?** Que será riquísimo ahora, pero menos miserable era cuando estaba más pobre que una rata.

Tú: En eso estoy de acuerdo. Cuanto más rico, más mezquino es.

Yo: No tienes que jurármelo. Está cada vez más tacaño.

Tú: Bueno, siempre lo fue. Más tacaño que una hormiga.

Yo: Y ahora no suelta ya ni un duro. Con él no se puede contar para nada.

Tú: Por eso está cada vez más solo también. ¡Más solo que la una!

Yo: Tampoco eso es nada nuevo. Siempre fue un egoista.

Tú: Es verdad, nunca fue amigo de nadie. Siempre estuvo solo.

Yo: Y ahora más aún, pues se cree que es el mejor del mundo. Poderoso caballero don dinero, ¿no?

Tú: Pues para mí es un don nadie.

Yo: ¡Pobre de quien cargue con él!   Ese, por muy millonario que sea ahora y por más rico que esté, no creo que haya quién lo aguante.

Tú: Estoy de acuerdo. Ese tío tan tacaño no puede gustarle a nadie, por más rico que sea. ¡Desgraciada la chica que caiga en sus garras!

Vocabulary and idioms:

Estar más solo que la una:	to be friendless
Ser un don nadie:	to be a nobody, to be of no importance
Más pobre que una rata:	as poor as a church mouse
Poderoso caballero don dinero:	lit: A powerful man is Mr. Money fig: Money is power

FRESCO/A:

MAS FRESCO QUE UNA LECHUGA

Yo:	¿Qué haces?
Tú:	Aquí estoy al fresco, sentado a la sombra. Aquí se está muy fresco. Aquí estoy muy fresquito.
Yo:	Sí, es verdad. El aire está fresco, y tú eres como el aire. ¡Muy fresco estás tú!
Tú:	Sí, es verdad. El aire es fresco, y tú eres como el aire, ¡Eres un fresco!

Vocabulary and Idioms:

Fresco:	cool, cold, fresh; fig: cheeky
Estar fresco: Ser un fresco:	to be cool, to be saucy to be an ill-mannered, cheeky, saucy, impertinent sort of person
¡Muy fresco estás tú!	to be a cool cheeky one; to be foolishly mistaken
Ser más fresco que una lechuga:	to be as cool as a cucumber
Estar al fresco:	to be in the open air

141

FRIO/A

TIRITANDO DE FRIO

Yo:
El aire era muy frío,
por eso estaba tan frío aquel crudo
amanecer de tiritones
y arrecido aliento.
El agua de la fuente estaba fría,
helada,
aquel día blanco de escarcha;
hasta la nieve de los cerros,
que ya de por sí es glacial y alba,
estaba más yerta,
más rabiosamente fría y blanca,
aquella mañana de hielo,
bella
como una navidad de sueño
y de juguetes de algodones.

Tú:
¿Y dónde está lo bello
en tu amanecer de tiritones?
El día era frío
y yo estaba esmorecido
muerto de frío y temblones,
tiritando de la cabeza a los pies,
como un gorrión desplumado.
Y todo lo demás es poesía barata,
un ripio,
y un cuento chino.
Y por más que quieras que sea navidad,
una navidad de lana blanca
de borrego,
como salgas a la calle,
te vas a pelar con ese aire mortal
de hoz de segar,
pues el día está helado;
y tú, aterido de frío,
poeta de pecho mocho y versos calvos.

Vocabulary and Idioms:

Estar tiritando:	to be shivering
Estar arrecido/esmorecido/ aterido:	to be numb/stiff with cold
Estar yerto/a:	to be stiff, rigid, numb; poetic: to be very cold
Te vas a pelar [de frío]:	fig: you're going to die [of cold]
Alba:	lit: dawn; alb (white cloth), poetic: white
Un ripio:	doggerel, empty words
Un cuento chino:	a cock-and-bull story
Hoz de segar:	sickle
Mocho:	not very hairy, shorn, close-cropped

ORGULLOSO/A

UN ORGULLOSO A MUCHA HONRA

Yo: Eres orgulloso.

Tú: ¡Y a mucha honra!

Yo: ¿Y estás orgulloso de ser orgulloso?

Tú: ¿Y por qué no? Si soy orgulloso, ¿por qué no voy a estar orgulloso de serlo?

Vocabulary:

Ser orgulloso/a: to be arrogant/conceited

Estar orgulloso/a de: to be proud of

CASADO/A:

¿CASADO Y CANSADO?

¿Casado?:

Yo: ¿Es usted casado?

Tú: Sí, soy casado. Soy un hombre casado y muy orgulloso que estoy de estar casado.

¿Cansado?:

Yo: ¿Estás casado?

Tú: Sí, estoy casado y sin solución.

Yo: ¿Estás cansado ya?

Tú: Ese es mi problema: que estoy cansado de estar casado.

Vocabulary:

Ser/Estar casado/a: to be married, See pp. 31-35.

CLARO/A:

¡PUES NO ESTA CLARO!

Yo: Si lo estoy viendo con estos dos ojos. Si lo veo y está tan claro como que tú estás vivo, ¿cómo puedo decir que no está claro?

Tú: Para ti todo es blanco y negro. Todo está más claro que el agua, ¿no?

Yo: Todo no, pero hay cosas clarísimas. Cosas que son tan claras como el que dos y dos son cuatro.

Tú: ¿Por ejemplo?

Yo: Pues que esta habitación es muy clara.

Tú: Pero apago la luz y... Como es de noche, cuando la luz está apagada, esta habitación está ya oscura.

Yo: ¡Qué inteligente estás!

Tú: ¡Qué inteligente soy!

Vocabulary:

See *ser/estar claro* pp. 68 and 70.
See *ser/estar inteligente* pp. 38-40.

CATOLICO/A:

¿MAS CATOLICO QUE EL PAPA?

Yo: Dicen que no es de cristiano el ser tan intransigente.

Tú: Pues en eso estamos de acuerdo. Pedro, entonces, debe de ser poco cristiano.

Yo: Yo diría que es más papista que el Papa.

Tú: Pues yo dudo que nadie pueda scr más papista que el Papa. Nadie es más católico que el Papa.

Yo: Pues precisamente porque es más papista que el Papa, Pedro no es muy católico.

Tú: ¿Tú qué quieres? ¿Quedarte conmigo?

Yo: Pero es verdad, ¿no?

Tú: ¿El que no es de cristiano el ser tan dogmático? ¿El ser tan intransigente?

Yo: Por supuesto que no. Ni es de católico tampoco.

Tú: ¿Que no?

Yo: Que sí. Que te lo digo yo. Además, estamos de acuerdo, ¿no? ¡Pedro es tan católico! Para él, todo es siempre blanco o negro.

Tú: ¿En qué estamos, entonces? ¿Pedro es o no es católico?

Yo: Tú dirás. Todavía va a misa todos los domingos. Si no, pregúntaselo tú mismo a él y ya verás cómo te dice que sí, que él es muy católico.

Tú:	Pues en eso sí que estás equivocado. Pedro ahora no está muy católico.
Yo:	¿Y por qué? ¿Es que ha dejado de ir a misa?
Tú:	No. Porque está con un resfriado horroroso.
Yo:	Desde luego, contigo no se puede hablar en serio.
Tú:	¡Y ahora te das cuenta!

Vocabulary and Idioms:

Ser más papista que el Papa:	to be dogmatic, intransigent
¿En qué estamos, entonces?:	What have we decided on then?
¿Tú qué quieres? ¿Quedarte conmigo?	Are you trying to make fun of me/make me look ridiculous?

Ser/estar católico see p. 40.

DIFICIL:

TODAVIA MAS DIFICIL

Yo: La vida está muy difícil.

Tú: Si hablaras con propiedad, dirías que la vida es muy difícil, y no que la vida está muy difícil.

Yo: Pues, hablando con propiedad, te vuelvo a repetir que la vida está muy difícil.

Tú: Que es muy difícil, querrás decir.

Yo: Pues estás equivocado. De sobra sé yo cómo es la vida. La vida siempre ha sido muy difícil y por supuesto que no va a cambiar ya.

Tú: Luego me estás dando la razón.

Yo: Pues no. Porque yo estoy en lo cierto cuando digo que, debido a la situación actual, la vida está ahora más difícil.

CACHONDO/A:

UN CACHONDO SIN GANAS DE CACHONDEO

Yo: Juan está cachondo, ¿no?

Tú: Juan siempre ha sido un cachondo. Pero hoy no está de cachondeo.

Yo: Yo no me refiero a si está o no está de broma, sino si está cachondo, si está de marcha.

Tú: Pues no, no está salido.

Yo: ¿Y cómo sabes que no está salido?

Tú: Porque no ves que está en casa, que no está fuera. Si estuviera salido, estaría por ahí... , tú sabes..

Yo: ¿Y eso qué es? Un chiste malo, ¿no...? Yo no te he preguntado si ha salido, sino si está salido.

Tú: Y yo te he dicho que no está salido, porque no ha salido.

Yo: ¡Muy cachondo estás tú hoy!

Tú: Eso sí que no. Yo sí que no estoy salido.

Vocabulary and Idioms:

Estar de cachondeo/de broma: to be in a joking mood (Also: see p. 61)

Estar de marcha: to be/feel randy

Cachondo/salido: see p. 58.

GORDO/A:

FINA ESTA GORDITA

Yo: Fina no es gorda.

Tú: Pero está algo gordita.

Yo: En verdad, siempre fue delgada.

Tú: Muy delgadita.

Yo: Pero desde que le dio por los dulces, no es que sea gorda ya, pero...

Tú: Sino que está algo gordita.

Vocabulary:

Fina: woman's name

Fino/a: thin, skinny; fig: a polite, courteous refined person

POLVO:

UN MIERCOLES DE CENIZA

Yo:　　　Estoy hecho polvo.

Tú:　　　Claro, como que es miércoles de ceniza. Recuerda, hombre, que eres polvo y en polvo te convertirás.

Yo:　　　Entonces tú también estarás hecho polvo, ¿no?

Tú:　　　Pues no. Yo todavía no he mordido el polvo.

Vocabulary and Idioms:

Estar hecho polvo:　　to be worn out, shattered, devastated

Miércoles de ceniza:　Ash Wednesday

Morder el polvo:　　　to bite the dust, to die

TONTO/A:

A CUAL MAS TONTO

Yo: No digo que seas tonto, sino que estás tonto.

Tú: Pues yo te digo a ti que no es que tú estés tonto, sino que lo eres.

CHAPTER SIX

Ser and *Estar* in Dialogue

VI

CONTENTS:

DE TAL PALO, TAL ASTILLA

María:	¿Cómo está Gonza?
Carmen:	Gonza es un verdadero gamberro, pero está muy simpático el muy pillín.
María:	Está igualito que su hermano, ¿verdad?
Carmen:	Sí, está tan alto como él, ¡Y eso que tiene dos años menos!
María:	Sí, que es verdad.
Carmen:	Dicen que es clavado a su padre.
María:	Pues sí, es igual que su padre. Va a ser tan alto y guapo como él.
Carmen:	¡Y simpático que es además!
María:	En eso también tiene a quién salir. De tal palo, tal astilla.

Vocabulary and Idioms:

Ser un gamberro: usually: to be a hooligan, lout;
but here: to be a little devil

Ser clavado a alguien: to be the spitting image of someone

De tal palo, tal astilla: a chip off the old block;
like father, like son.

EL MISMO ROLLO DE SIEMPRE

Madre:	Juan, ¡quieres callarte, que eres un loro!
Hijo:	Mamá, es que...
Madre:	Te digo que te calles de una vez. Que estés callado al menos un rato. ¡Que no seas pesado!
Hijo:	Y ¿por qué no me dejas ir al cine?
Madre:	Ay, hijo mío, ¡qué pesado estás! Estás de un latoso y pesado que me traes frita. ¡Pero frita de verdad!
Hijo:	Anda, mamá, déjame.
Madre:	Cuando digo yo que tú estás hoy pesado con ganas. Pues porque ya te lo he dicho bien claro. ¿Es que eres sordo? Te he dicho que no, ¿no?
Hijo:	Pero si a Javi...
Madre:	¿Es que quieres que te lo repita otra vez? ¿Estás sordo?
Hijo:	Por favor, mamá, a Javi su madre le ha dado permiso. ¿Por qué a mí...
Madre:	Por amor de Dios, Juan, ¡estáte callado! ¡Déjame en paz! Mira que estás hoy insoportable, ¿eh?
Hijo:	Pues su madre...
Madre:	¿Todavía sigues? ¡Dale que dale! Desde luego eres un rollo. A veces, hijo mío, ¡eres de un insoportable! ¡Qué testarudo eres! Pero ¡qué cabezota! Te he dicho que no.

Hijo:	Anda, mamá, qué trabajo te cuesta. Si es que...
Madre:	Se acabó de una vez. ¿Eres tonto o qué? ¡Que no!, y no seas más pesado.
Hijo:	Y si te prometo...
Madre:	¡Estás tonto! ¿Qué te pasa? ¡No y no! Y no seas más tonto, si no quieres que te castigue. ¿Es que no atiendes a razones? ¿Estás torpe o qué?
Hijo:	Pues no es justo.
Madre:	Ay, hijo mío. Estoy de ti ya hasta la coronilla.
Hijo:	Javi sí, y yo en cambio....
Madre:	Desde luego eres bien torpe, ¿eh?...Cuando seas tan obediente como Javi, a lo mejor entonces. Mucho tienes tú que aprender de Javi antes. Ojalá fueras tú como Javi! Javi es más bueno que el pan, él sí que es un pedazo de pan, pero tú... Cuando tú seas tan bueno como Javi, entonces hablaremos.
Hijo:	Sí, eso, que te crees tú que Javi es una mosquita muerta.
Madre:	Ya está bien. Estáte callado.
Hijo:	Que Javi es...
Madre:	Ni una palabra más.
Hijo:	Que...
Madre:	¡Sanseacabó!

Vocabulary and Idioms:

Un rollo:	a rolling pin, a roll; fig: boring, tedious
Ser un rollo:	to be a nuisance
El mismo rollo de siempre:	the same old boring story; here also: to be heavy-going, a nuisance
Ser pesado:	to be heavy
Ser [un] pesado:	to be a nuisance, heavy-going (WHAT-NESS)
Estar pesado:	to be a nuisance, heavy-going (HOW-NESS)
Estar de un latoso/pesado:	to be a nuisance, to make a nuisance of oneself
Traer frito/a a alguien:	to drive someone mad, to make someone angry
La coronilla:	the crown of the head
Estar hasta la coronilla:	to be fed-up to the back teeth
Ser más bueno que el pan:	to be as good as gold
Ser un pedazo de pan:	to be a very nice, good person, to be a saint
Ser una mosquita muerta:	to look as if butter would not melt in one's mouth

FEA COMO EL HAMBRE

Luisa:	¿Qué te pasa?
Ana:	¿A mí?
Luisa:	Sí, a ti. Tu cara está blanca como la pared. ¡Estás tan seria hoy!
Ana:	Nada, ¿Por qué?
Luisa:	Pues ni que estuvieras de luto.
Ana:	Pues no se me ha muerto nadie.
Luisa:	Entonces serás tú la muerta. ¡Estás lista ya, chica!
Ana:	No será ésa yo.
Luisa:	No hay más que ver tu cara. Es de pena. La cara de una muerta.
Ana:	Pues no estoy muerta aún.
Luisa:	Estarás, entonces, con un pie en la sepultura. Tú estás ya para el arrastre, chica.
Ana:	Todavía estoy bien viva.
Luisa:	Sí, sí. ¡Bien vivita y coleando estás tú! Por mucho que te empeñes en disimularlo, algo te pasa. Tú cara es de risa.
Ana:	Cuántas veces te voy a decir que no me pasa nada. Que estoy bien. Que estoy normal.
Luisa:	¿Normal tú? Vamos, que no estoy ciega. ¡Vaya cara que tienes hoy! ¡Cuando te digo yo que eres la funeraria en persona!
Ana:	No estarás pesada, ¿verdad? ¡¿No serás aguafiestas?!

162

Luisa:	No lo tomes a mal, ¿eh? Era sólo una broma. Sólo para que no estés tan seria. Que estás muy fea, mujer, cuando estás triste.
Ana:	Ahora va a resultar que no sólo estoy triste, sino que soy muy fea.
Luisa:	No, no. Yo no he dicho que tú seas fea, sino que estás fea, ¡que no es lo mismo!
Ana:	Bueno, corta el rollo, ¿no?
Luisa:	Que quede claro.
Ana:	¿El qué?
Luisa:	Pues el que tú no eres fea. Pero, hija, tu cara está hoy tan pálida y demacrada que da pena. Si estuvieras maquillada, lo podrías disimular, pero estás de un feo hoy con esa mirada de hambre...
Ana:	Pues has metido la pata de nuevo. No estoy a régimen.
Luisa:	Seguro que no lo estás. Pero tu cara está tan chupada y descolorida que verdaderamente cualquiera diría que estás muerta de hambre.
Ana:	¡Tú serás la hambrienta!
Luisa:	Está visto que no sabes aguantar bromas.
Ana:	No estoy para bromas, así que corta.
Luisa:	¡Eh, eh , eh! , que yo estaba sólo bromeando.
Ana:	¡Y yo en broma también! ¿Vale?
Luisa:	Sí, sí, ¡vale!

Vocabulary and Idioms:

Estar blanca como la pared:	to be as white as a sheet
Estar de luto:	to be in mourning
Estar listo/a:	to be ready
¡Estás lista, chica!:	here: You're ready for the cemetery, girl!
Es de pena:	it's pitiful
Estar para el arrastre:	to be ready for the scrap heap, to be done for
Ser vivo/a:	to be lively
Ser un/una muerto/a:	to be a corpse
Estar vivo/a:	to be alive
Estar muerto/a:	to be dead (see pp. 99)
Estar vivito y coleando:	to be alive and kicking; to be hale and hearty
Ser la funeraria en persona:	to be the funeral parlour personified
Ser [un/una] aguafiestas:	to be a killjoy, wet blanket, spoilsport
Estar a régimen:	to be on a diet
Corta el rollo:	Shut-up, stop talking rubbish; Cut the crap

UN PEZ QUE NO SABE NADAR

Pepe: Juan nada que es un pez.

Carlos: ¡Y qué! ¡Ojalá tuviera yo la piscina que él tiene!

Pepe: Eso es verdad. La piscina es fabulosa.

Carlos: ¡Así cualquiera! Con una piscina así, también estaría yo hecho un pez. ¿Te imaginas? Estaría todo el santo día metido dentro del agua, y...

Pepe: Pues tú, ni así. Seguro que ni aun así nadarías como Juan.

Carlos: ¡No seas idiota! Si yo tuviera una piscina como la suya, me apuesto lo que quieras que yo sería mejor que él.

Pepe: ¿Tú mejor que Juan?

Carlos: ¿Que no..? Estaría tirado. Si fuera ésa mi piscina, yo nadaría como un pez.

Pepe: O como un besugo.

Carlos: ¡Tú sí que eres un besugo!

Pepe: ¡Besugo, tú! ¡Tú, que te crees que el nadar está chupado!.... Fíjate en Paco. Se pasa todo el verano en la playa y sin embargo está pez, ¡como tú!, completamente pez en natación.

Carlos: ¡Y qué! No me vas a comparar tú a mí con Paco, ¿verdad? Porque ése no sabe nada de nada. Ese está pegado en todo. ¡Pues no es torpe Paco!

Pepe: No te lo niego.

Carlos: ¡Paco es más bruto que un arado!

Pepe: ¡Qué va! Para bruto, Rafa. Ese sí que está pegado en todo. Por algo es el último de la clase.

Carlos: Pues sí que te estás luciendo tú hoy. ¡Vaya chorrada! Ni que estuvieras descubriendo América, chico. ¡Ni que fueras tonto del culo! Tú estarás el primero en la clase, pero sales con cada majadería... ¡Como si yo no supiera que Rafa está el último! ¡El último en todo!

Pepe: Pues, ¡no! El último en todo, no. Rafa será el último de la clase, ¡de acuerdo! pero sabe más inglés que tú y yo juntos.

Carlos: ¡Y qué!. No tiene mérito. Si él no está pez en inglés, es sólo porque su abuela es inglesa y ha ido muchas veces a Inglaterra.

Pepe: ¿Que no tiene mérito? ¿Y qué me dices del padre de Juan, por ejemplo?

Carlos: ¿Qué?

Pepe: Pues que mucha piscina y, sin embargo, no sabe nadar. El mismo Juan nos los dijo, ¿te acuerdas?

Carlos: ¿Y a qué viene esto? Otra de tus salidas inteligentes, ¿no?

Pepe: Pues que el padre de Juan será un pez gordo (sí, todo lo gordo e importante que quieras), pero está pez en natación, como Paco.

Carlos: Pues vaya majadería, ¿eh?.

Pepe: Pues que probablemente tú, aunque fueras a Inglaterra cada verano, todavía no sabrías ni decir thank you.

Carlos: ¡Muy gracioso estás tú hoy!

Pepe: ¿Y ahora te das cuenta? ¿Qué creías tú? Que tú eras el único gracioso, ¿verdad?

Carlos: ¡Menos guasa!

Vocabulary and Idioms:

Estar pez en:	to be useless, hopeless at
Estar pegado en:	not to have a clue about, to know absolutely nothing about
Estar tirado:	to be very easy; to be a piece of cake, a cinch
Besugo:	fish similar to sea bream or red snapper
Ser un besugo:	to be an idiot
Ser un pez gordo:	to be a big shot, a bigwig, an important person
¡Menos guasa!:	Stop fooling around!; Less cheek!

FELIZ EN EL SEPTIMO CIELO

Lola: ¿Dónde está María?

Josefa: ¿Dónde quieres que esté? Como siempre, ¿no? Esa niña estará como siempre. Seguro, en el séptimo cielo. Feliz en su mundo.

Lola: ¡Ojalá pudiéramos estar nosotras también en el séptimo cielo ya! Pero, hija, estamos tan ajetreadas todo el santo día. María, en cambio, bien que sabe despistarse y escurrir el bulto.

Josefa: Pues mejor que siga estando en Babia o dondequiera que esté ahora, porque en verdad es más un estorbo que una ayuda. Además, ésa no cambia ya. Lo mejor es ignorarla, digo yo.

Lola: No, si ya lo sé. Demasiado bien sé yo que esa niña se va a pasar en Babia ya toda su vida.

Josefa: Tú lo has dicho. No estés preocupada, pues.

Lola: Pero qué pena, hija, que esté siempre en las nubes, ¿verdad? Siempre en las musarañas.

Josefa: Acéptalo. Es una despistada, ¡eso es todo!

Lola: Sí, una distraída. ¡Eso será todo!

Josefa: No es nada nuevo, ¿no?

Lola: No, claro, Siempre lo ha sido. Y ahora estará por ahí, como siempre... ¡Vete tú a saber dónde estará esa niña ahora!

Vocabulary and Idioms:

Estar en las nubes:	to be in the clouds, to be daydreaming
Estar [pensando] en las musarañas:	to be daydreaming, to be lost in one's thoughts
Estar despistado:	to be absent-minded, to be daydreaming
Estar distraído/a:	to be absent-minded, to be daydreaming
Babia:	a mountainous region of Leon
Estar en Babia:	to be daydreaming, to be wrapped-up in one's own thoughts
Estar ajetreado/a:	to be busy, to slave away
Ser un estorbo:	to be a nuisance, a hindrance
Ser un distraído/a:	to be an absent-minded person/a daydreamer
Ser un despistado/a:	to be an absent-minded person

MAS CIEGO QUE UN TOPO

Rafael: Pues está tan claro que no me explico que no lo veas. Debes de estar ciego.

Antonio: Te digo que no es posible que María sea así.

Rafael: ¿Que no? Pues entonces, eres ciego. ¡Más ciego que un topo!

Antonio: No soy ciego, porque todavía tengo dos ojos y veo con ellos perfectamente. No como tú, que necesitas gafas.

Rafael: No tendrás gafas, pero tú no ves ni tres en un burro.

Antonio: ¿Quién? ¿Yo?... Yo no estoy ciego. ¿No ves que me doy perfecta cuenta de que eres un mentiroso? ¡Que eres el mayor embustero de este mundo!

Rafael: ¡Y tú, un majadero! Tú podrás ver mejor que yo, pero si no te das cuenta de que María no es de fiar, es que eres ciego de nacimiento. ¡Allá tú con tu ceguera!

Vocabulary and Idioms:

Un topo: a mole

Más ciego que un topo: as blind as a bat

No ver ni tres en un burro: to be as blind as a bat; not to see something even if it is staring one in the face.

UNAS GAFAS CON CULO DE BOTELLA

Angela: El pobrecillo está cegato perdido.

Beatriz: Sí, ya lo sé. Me da pena verlo con esas gafas. ¿Te has fijado en los cristales que lleva?

Angela: Como que son más gordos que el culo de una botella.

Beatriz: Pues como siga así, pronto va a estar ya ciego del todo.

Angela: Sí, es una verdadera pena.

Idiom: Estar cegato perdido: to be hopelessly short-sighted/poor-sighted

EN MEDIO DE LA VIOLENCIA

Julia: La situación fue de lo más violenta. Créeme, fue violentísima. Y como te puedes imaginar, yo estaba muy violenta también.

Cristina: Menos mal que no estaba Juan, pues ¡con lo violento que es!

Julia: Desde luego. Si hubiera estado Juan, todo habría sido más violento aún.

Cristina: Y tú habrías estado más violenta, ¿verdad?

Julia: Bueno, en verdad... Quizá no. Juan está ya mucho mejor. Desde que ya no está en el paro, bebe menos y parece más sosegado. Sí, está menos violento. No creo, pues, que lo tomase tan mal como para que llegara a usar de la violencia.

Cristina: Pues yo no lo creo. La última vez que lo vi, estaba con una zorra encima gordísima y ¡estaba de un violento el muy fiera!

Vocabulary and Idioms:

Una zorra: vixen;
fig: a cunning person; a prostitute; drunkenness

Estar con una zorra encima gordísima:
lit: to have a fat female fox on top of one;
fig: to be blind drunk

Ser violento/a: to be violent

Estar violento/a: to be embarrassed

172

DOS ABUELITAS A LA ANTIGUA USANZA:

ESCENA I:

Abuelita 2:	Quien va a ser un hombrón es tu nieto Tomás.
Abuelita 1:	Sí, que es verdad. Está muy crecidito. ¡Qué buen mozo que está, ¿verdad?!
Abuelita 2:	¡Y buen chico que es también!
Abuelita 1:	De eso ya no estoy yo tan segura. No es buen estudiante. Tampoco es muy obediente. Según su madre, está demasiado patoso y por lo visto es un ganso en el colegio. Ese niño va ser un problema.
Abuelita 2:	Pues yo creía que no era así. ¡Qué desilusión, hija!
Abuelita 1:	En cambio, mi nieto Jorge ése sí que es un niño modelo.
Abuelita 2:	Sí que es verdad. Conmigo es siempre muy educado. Para mí, de todos mis nietos, está feo decirlo pero el preferido es Toñete.
Abuelita 1:	¿Cómo está?
Abuelita 2:	Pues cada día está más mono. El niño es monísimo.
Abuelita 1:	La que tiene mérito es su madre. La pobrecilla lo está educando de maravilla, siendo como es viuda.
Abuelita 2:	Sí, que es verdad. Mérito tiene, estando como está viuda desde que Toñete era una criaturita en pañales. Demasiado bien que lo está sacando adelante.

Abuelita 1:	Yo le tengo lástima.
Abuelita 2	Muchas gracias que le doy yo a Dios. La criatura está muy bien educada. Esperemos que no se estropee más tarde, que no vaya a dar nunca con malas compañías. Yo mucho que se lo repito a mi hija: Que tenga cuidado. Que no sea débil con él por aquello de que no tiene padre el pobrecillo.
Abuelita 1:	Es cierto, hija. Lo que tiene que hacer es no consentirlo nunca. No es bueno. Ese fue el problema con el hijo de Juana, ¿te acuerdas? Aquel niño estuvo siempre demasiado consentido. ¡Bien que lo decía yo!
Abuelita 2:	Sí, que es verdad.
Abuelita 1:	Y ya sabemos cómo ha terminado. Ese niño es hoy un gandul y un vago. ¡Pobre madre! Ese niño debe de ser ahora un verdadero dolor para ella.
Abuelita 2:	No creo que vaya a ser ése el caso con Toñete. Toñete, gracias a Dios, es una monada de niño. ¡Es tan educadito! Y monísimo que es el angelito.
Abuelita 1:	Yo siempre he dicho que es normal que los niños sean un poco caprichosos, y hasta algo consentidos, pero sólo mientras sean muy pequeñitos, claro. Pero no me gusta tampoco que estén tan mimados.
Abuelita 2:	A mí tampoco. Por eso quiero yo tanto a mi Toñete. Toñete es un encanto de niño. No es nada mimado. Bueno, algo mimado sí lo está. Pero, como dices, es normal que lo esté un poquito, ¿verdad? Demasiado poco, digo yo, siendo como es hijo único y sin padre.

Vocabulary and Idioms:

Estar patoso:	to be heavy-going, a nuisance
Estar consentido:	to be spoilt
Ser un ganso:	to be sloppy, foolishly indolent, stupid
Ser un gandul:	to be an idler, lazy person
Ser una monada de niño:	to be a lovely boy

ESCENA II:

Abuelita 1: ¿Y qué me dices del varón que tiene mi hija Encarnita?

Abuelita 2: Ayer precisamente lo vi cuando lo llevaba su padre al colegio. Hay que ver lo grande que está para su edad.

Abuelita 1: Y lo guapetón que está también el muy pillín. ¡Es de un guapo!

Abuelita 2: Sí, que está hermoso. Tiene muy buen color. Se ve que está muy sano.

Abuelita 1: Además es un niño muy sano también. No es nada malicioso. Sí, no tiene ninguna doblez ese niño.

Abuelita 2: Pues si tú conocieras a mi ahijada Angelita, ésa sí que es buenísima. Ya te digo, tiene un corazón que es de oro. Y es graciosa la chiquilla. Y muy simpática que es también. Ya lo creo que sí.

Abuelita 1: Para mí, además de Toñete, mi ahijado Alejandro es el que está para comérselo. Está travieso con ganas. Pero también ¡es de un simpático y listo! Bueno, en verdad, es un niño muy bueno Tampoco es travieso en realidad, porque dice su madre que en la guardería es bueno, pero bueno, que es la criatura. Lo que pasa es que está en la edad de las travesuras y ¡está de un travieso! ¡Está monísimo, de verdad!

Abuelita 2:	¿Y qué me dices tú de mi ahijada Rosarito? Ya sabes que siempre fue monísima. Pues ahora está guapísima. Todo lo que te diga es poco. Esa niña es igualita que su madre. Su pelo es rubio, el cutis es de un rosado precioso, y sus ojos, ¿qué te voy a decir?, son grandes como dos... como...
Abuelita 1:	Pues yo, aunque la niña fuera guapísima, vamos, la más guapa de todo el barrio, no se lo estaría diciendo todo el tiempo. Hay que tener mucho cuidado. Si no quieres, claro, que después sea una niña presumida y tonta.
Abuelita 2:	¿Mi ahijada? ¡Qué va! No va a ser ese el caso. Es una niña. Y como cualquier niña de su edad, como tus nietas por ejemplo, está un poco presumida y mimosa, pero eso tampoco es malo, ¿no?
Abuelita 1:	De mis nietas, gracias a Dios, ninguna ha salido presumida. Ninguna hay que sea coqueta.
Abuelita 2:	Mis nietas tampoco.

Vocabulary and Idioms:

Estar sano/a:	to be healthy
Ser un niño muy sano:	to be a good, wholesome boy
Doblez:	duplicity, double-dealing
No tener doblez: here:	to be an ingenuous, sincere person

ESCENA III:

Abuelita 1:	Mi nieto Rafa es ya un hombre.
Abuelita 2:	Pues ojalá mi nieto estuviera ya hecho un hombre. A mi Julito todavía le quedan muchos años para que yo lo pueda ver hecho todo un hombre. Ya veremos si para entonces estoy yo todavía en este mundo.
Abuelita 1:	Claro que sí, mujer.
Abuelita 2:	Todavía es muy pequeño, y yo ... Yo estoy ya bastante torpe.
Abuelita 1:	No digas eso. Además, tu Julito está ya en el colegio.
Abuelita 2:	Y pronto estará en la edad del pavo también, claro. Pero yo no estoy ya para trotes. No creo yo que esté viva para entonces.
Abuelita 1:	¡Pues no tienes tú todavía mucho que rodar por este barrio! Tú estás todavía muy bien. Ya quisieran muchas estar como tú.
Abuelita 2:	Pues yo te aseguro que, como se ponga mi Julito con la edad del pavo igualito que su hermana Carmencita, acabarán mandándome de una vez al otro mundo.
Abuelita 1:	No digas esas cosas, mujer. No está bien.

Abuelita 2:	Porque qué pena, hija. Que no, que no hay manera de que Carmencita acabe de salir de la edad del pavo. Y créeme, ¡está de un inaguantable! Me está dando cada disgusto esa chiquilla. Dirás que son cosas de la edad, pero lo que más me duele es que mi Carmencita sea tan arisca.
Abuelita 1:	No le des importancia, mujer. Mi nieta Paquita también estuvo muy arisca hasta hace bien poco. Ya verás cómo, cuando menos lo pienses, se le habrá pasado y estará ya igual que mi nieta. Paquita es un encanto ahora. ¡Está tan cariñosa conmigo!
Abuelita 2:	Conmigo tu nieta siempre ha estado cariñosísima.
Abuelita 1:	Porque se te ha olvidado lo tonta que estuvo cuando estaba en la edad del pavo.
Abuelita 2:	No, de verdad. Para mí, tu nieta siempre ha sido una niña muy cariñosa. Un encanto de niña.
Abuelita 2:	Sí, pero también pasó por la edad del pavo. Y estuvo muy antipática y chocante conmigo. Como lo está ahora contigo tu nieta Carmencita. Ya se le pasará a ella también.
Abuelita 1:	Ya veremos.
Abuelita 2:	Seguro que sí, mujer.

Vocabulary and Idioms:

Torpe:	clumsy, dim-witted, slow
Estar torpe:	here: to be slow (through old age)
Estar en la edad del pavo:	fig: to be going through the awkward years of adolescence.
No estar para trotes:	not to be up to it anymore
No estoy ya para trotes:	I can't go running around like I used to
Ser un encanto:	to be a lovely person

CHAPTER SEVEN

Ser and *Estar*—
The Cornerstone of Creative Language

VII

CONTENTS:

LOS TRES JUANES:

I

JUAN EL MALAS PULGAS

Juan siempre fue un poco raro pero, desde que le dio por aupar el codo, está como un cencerro. Pena me da de que esté ya tan disparatado y, para colmo de desgracia, más molesto y achacoso que un viejo carcamal. Claro, con eso de que todo se le va en beber y nada en comer, cada día está más chungo. El pobrecillo está pocho con ganas y con más malas pulgas que un chucho callejero... Y así se pasa las horas muertas: hundido en la butaca, en bata, con la boina encajada hasta las cejas, una bufanda reliada al cuello, enroscado como un gato refunfuñón. Allí está Juan, hecho un trapo, ora durmiendo la mona, ora cargando a cuestas con todos sus achaques y dolores. No es que sea muy viejo, que todavía no ha cumplido ni los cincuenta; pero está viejísimo y todo él lleno de arrugas. Como un higo seco. Lo peor no es que esté ya pasado y totalmente calvo (pues Juan es calvo desde que perdió el pelo con la tiña cuando todavía era un buen mozo), ni el que esté tan chupado o chocho (porque en eso da pena ver al triste con lo altivo y gallardo que fue antaño), sino que está de un irritable y quisquilloso que verdaderamente despide a la gente. No es de extrañar, pues, que quien no lo conozca, crea (y con razón) que Juan no es más que un viejo cascarrabias. Un carrañoso. Un abuelito gruñón. Para él, el más mínimo ruido es molesto. El otro día, por ejemplo, fui a hacerle una visita y porque sin querer, al ir a cerrar la puerta, se me fue la mano y dio un portazo, se enfadó como si fuese un niño con rabieta. Y ya estuvo molesto conmigo para el resto de la tarde. Pero eso no es nada. Más molesto se puso el día cuando su ahijado que es tan imprudente (bueno, el angelito apenas si tiene cinco años), le preguntó que por qué era calvo. Juan le regañó a la pobre criatura, diciéndole que era un mal educado, que hay que ver lo mal educado que estaba, que si no le enseñaban educación a los niños de hoy, que bien podría aprender de él a ser educado, y yo qué sé cuántas cosas más... Y para colmo de desgracia (pues iría a provocar una carcajada prematuramente maliciosa en el ahijado), no se le ocurrió otra cosa que chillarle que él no era calvo y que, si estaba calvo, era sólo porque se había afeitado la cabeza, que eso era todo: su cabeza estaba afeitada porque estaba malo. ¡Qué se habría creído el muy indino!, su cabeza no era una bola de billar, ¡vamos con el niño!

Vocabulary and Idioms:

Pulga:	flea
Estar con/Tener malas pulgas:	to be touchy, irritable
Un chucho callejero:	a stray, mangy dog
Un cencerro:	a cowbell
Estar como un cencerro:	to be as mad as a hatter
Estar disparatado:	to be crazy, mad, out of control
Estar achacoso:	to be ailing, sickly, complaining

Un viejo carcamal:	an old wreck, crock
Estar chungo:	to be ill, off colour, sickly, depressed, low
Estar pocho:	to be overripe, rotten, soft, soggy; fig: depressed, gloomy; not well, off colour
Estar ya pasado:	to be past its sell by date; to be off
Estar hecho un trapo:	to feel rotten, to feel good for nothing
Estar chupado:	to look gaunt, drawn
Estar chocho:	to be doddery, senile
Ser molesto:	to be trying, annoying
Estar molesto:	to be annoyed; to have some discomfort
Estar molesto [con alguien]:	to be cross/annoyed with someone
Aupar/Empinar el codo:	to drink heavily, to booze

II

UN DON JUAN BARBILAMPIÑO

Dicen que Juan es todo un hombre, pero en verdad nunca lo ha sido. Juan es sólo un niño con pantalones largos. No es que todavía sea un niño, pues es ya casi cuarentón. El problema con Juan es que está aún tan verde e inmaduro como cuando era un pollito que, en cuanto lo echaban al corral, se ponía a cacarear. Como Dios no lo remedie, lleva carrera de ser un don Juan barbilampiño, con la cresta levantada y voz de melifluo sacristán.

Y se doctorará en soltería. Y como buen solterón empedernido, presumirá de ser un matón con las mujeres. Y sin embargo, ni la beata más desganada de la congregación se dejaría jamás seducir por este don Juan barbilampiño. Y es que por mucha toga y birrete de doctor que se engalane, por más que su cresta esté levantada en alto como si fuera una antorcha de atleta o una palma de procesión de Domingo de Ramos, demasiado bien que saben todas las comadronas del lugar que este don Juan no es más que un bachiller estancado en su pubertad.

Es ley de vida. Muy pronto pasarán los años por él, y su andar estará ya viejo y encorvado, y sus ojos no sabrán distinguir más entre lo que es una manzana o una uva pasa. Y sin embargo, allá irá él arrastrando todavía sus pies en pos de las mujeres como si fueran un plato de lentejas que estuviesen muy buenas o un bollito muy rico, mojado en chocolate: agonioso por probar un día la fruta prohibida que nunca había estado a su alcance.

187

Y allá iba don Juan el barbilampiño. Como un garduño. Rastreando la mirada. Aquella mirada tan suya que siempre fuera baja, pero que con los años estaba ya totalmente tirada por los suelos. Una mirada que presumía de ser noble, pero que era a todas luces rastrera y cegata, como la de una comadreja o la de un escarabajo pelotero. Incapaz de ver que por encima de ella siempre había un cielo azul. Y el azul de aquel cielo era un azul limpio. Un azul siempre puro. Siempre deslumbrante.

Y como a todos, le llegará a él también la hora. La hora que estaba escrita en las rayas de su mano. Y Juan morirá siendo viejo, tal vez ya octogenario y matusaleno. Pero por más años que le fuera a tocar llevarse consigo a la tumba, no podrá arrastrar con él más que un montón de huesos y años verdes. Aquellos muchos años, que cumplió cuando todavía era un ser vivo. Años que fueron todos iguales. Años repetidos, copiados de cuando era un pollito y se ponía a cacarear en medio de un corral de gallinas. Años que los estuvo cacareando toda su vida, jugando a ser hombre.

Y se lo llevarán al camposanto. Y sellarán su vida con una losa. Y en la losa estará escrito el siguiente epitafio:

"Aquí yace Juan, el que los mortales llamaron don Juan el barbilampiño, hijo bastardo de los Tenorios, al que le llegara su hora siendo como era una fruta inmadura, un viejo verde de por vida, por siempre verde."

Vocabulary and Idioms:

Verde:	green
Estar verde:	to be green, fig: to be immature, unripe
Ser un viejo verde:	dirty old man; here also: an old man who is still immature
Ser un matón:	to be a bully
Ser un matón [con las mujeres]	to be a lady-killer
Estar desganado:	to have no appetite, to lack interest; here: to be frustrated
Estar buena:	to be tasty, dishy
Un bollito:	a little bun, roll; fig: an attractive, pretty female, a real dish
Ser un bollito:	to be dishy

III

DON JUAN, UN MADRILEÑO DE PURA CASTA

Don Juan es de Madrid, pero no está en Madrid más. Desde hace ya más de medio siglo, por razones de destino y matrimonio (y no por su santa voluntad) está separado de su Madrid. Y sin embargo, en sus cincuentaitantos años de penar por tierras de villanos, Madrid jamás ha dejado (ni por asomo) de estar en el centro de sus entrañas. Siempre muy adentro, como si fuera el aliento que le estuviera dando el soplo de vida... Y mientras le queden todavía otoños por arrastrar a este don Juan, Madrid seguirá siendo el centro de todo su ser. Por algo, Madrid está escrito en la rayas de su mano, grabado a fuego lento. Y no habrá ya quien se lo fuere a arrancar de las carnes.

Ya bien que se lo auguró el ama, en tono muy de chulapa (o acaso de gitana que le estuviera echando la buenaventura), el mismo día que un mal viento se llevó a su Juan, con su flamante título de Señor Juez bajo el brazo, a tierras de rústicos, tierras de infieles:

Madrid es tu ombligo, criatura. Contigo te lo llevas, bien atado a tu barriga, para que jamás villano alguno te lo fuere a robar.

Don Juan es madrileño de alto abolengo. Un madrileño pura raza, con sabor añejo, del mejor mosto. Y madrileño será siempre hasta que se nos muera, llevándose su Madrid consigo a la tumba, bien apretado en el puño de la mano. Si sale Madrid en la conversación, que nadie le toque su Madrid, porque Madrid y él son uña y carne. Y bien orgulloso que está don Juan de su Madrid, pues por algo es suyo. Suyo sólo. Como si le hubiera tocado en la lotería el gordo. Como si se lo hubieran puesto los Reyes Magos. Madrid es su patria chica. Madrid, su capital grande.

Si hay un madrileño en destierro que pueda permitirse el lujo de ser presumido, es este don Juan de mirada altiva y cuerpo gallardo. Un madrileño de pura cepa, a la antigua usanza, como bien lo van pregonando a los cuatro vientos su figura castiza y su voz de la más exacta dicción. Su andar es garboso, de pasos acompasados. Su mirada es siempre aristócrata, siempre enhiesta.

Y las viejas de aquel pueblecito de rústicos, al verle pasar tan galán y pavoneado, cuchichean muy apretadas, en un corro de luto y mantones negros, que don Juan es un soberbio, que no hay ningún don Juan en toda la tierra que sea más soberbio y ufano que este madrileño de pura casta. Y en verdad no estarían muy equivocadas, si no fuera porque su soberbia es sólo fruto de aquella lozanía que le da el haber nacido en el viejo Madrid: Que en él no es pecado, sino una virtud y un privilegio reservado sólo a aquellos elegidos por los hados para proclamar las honras de un glorioso antaño. Por eso, que enhorabuena sea este don Juan un caballero ufano. Razón tiene él para ser más tieso que un palo seco. El paso de los años jamás logrará agacharle la mirada, pues bien que sabe él que (por muy alejado que esté de su Madrid) más allá del horizonte le está llamando su patria chica, su capital grande. Y así, fiel a su sino, cuando sale a pasear cuesta arriba, camino de la ermita, muy consciente que es este apuesto caballero de que en verdad está sacando de paseo a su Madrid. Y allá va don Juan, con su Madrid de la mano, como si fuera un juguete que arrastrara por las calles, para que todos los demás mortales le estén envidiosos. Y don Juan está satisfecho. Y don Juan está bien orgulloso. Muy ufano que está don Juan porque en todo Colmenar de la Frontera sólo uno, él, es don Juan el madrileño.

La fortuna, o malafortuna, quiso que lo destinaran a Colmenar de la Frontera cuando aún era joven y lozano, y que allí estuviese de juez hasta que no le quedara ya más cana en el pelo. Y allí está todavía, jubilado ya de sus menesteres de justicia, pero con su Madrid siempre a cuestas, cargando con su peso con la misma esbeltez de sus años de galán casamentero. Allí, en aquel publecito andaluz que será todo lo bonito y de algodón que quieran pintárselo, pero que jamás será de piedra sólida como su Madrid. Que nadie se atreva, pues, a compararle este pueblo blanco, que está hecho de sol y cal, con aquella ciudad con pedestal de roca, cuna de santos y héroes, la cual será por siempre el corazón y ombligo de su alma. Aquello que le hace a él ser un madrileño de pura casta.

Don Juan el madrileño le pusieron por mote los colmeneros, y muy orgulloso que está él de su apodo. Título que, por cierto, está haciéndole justicia, y que prefiere al de Señor Juez. Jueces hay muchos, pero madrileños de pura casta sólo un ramillete de privilegiados. Al menos así se lo está recordando machacón cada mañana, mientras se está vistiendo para salir a la calle. Y don Juan se está mirando al espejo. Y se aprieta el nudo de la corbata. Y se asegura de que sus hombros y espalda estén, también hoy, bien enderezados. Y más tieso ya que una jirafa, estando como estaba tan consciente hoy como antaño de su madrileñismo a ultranza, abre la puerta para encarar una vez más aquella tierra de villanos, con todo el empaque de un gentilhombre.

Y allá va don Juan con más años ya que Matusalén, cuesta arriba, sin arrastrar los pies ni agachar la mirada, con su Madrid siempre muy en alto: capa negra, traje blanco, bastón de mando más que cayado de viejo, cuello duro, recién almidonado, y sombrero de paja, viva copia de aquel madrileño de pura casta que llegara por primera vez a Colmenar de la Frontera.

Vocabulary and Idioms:

Ser de pura casta/raza:	a thoroughbred, to be of pure breed/pedigree
Ser de pura cepa:	a thoroughbred, to be of good stock
Años de penar:	years of suffering
Tierras de villanos/ rústicos//infieles:	land of peasants/rustics/infidels
Quedarle a uno tadavía otoños por arrastrar:	to have years still to live
Una chulapa:	a woman from the lower section of Madrid
Echar la buenaventura:	to tell someone his fortune
Ser madrileño de alto abolengo:	to be a Madrilenean of long/high lineage
Del mejor mosto:	lit: of the best must; fig: of the finest pedigree

Ser uña y carne:	to be hand in glove/as thick as thieves
Tocarle a uno el gordo:	to win the big prize, hit the jackpot
Los Reyes Magos:	The Three Wise Men; equivalent of Santa Claus
Enhiesto/a:	upright, erect
Ser presumido/a:	to be conceited, a show-off
Ser (un) soberbio/a:	to be arrogant, haughty, proud
Ser ufano/a:	to be proud of oneself
Estar ufano/a:	to be proud (HOWNESS)
Ser más tieso que un palo seco:	to be as stiff as a poker
Estar jubilado/a:	to be retired
Menesteres de justicia:	legal duties, occupation
Los colmeneros:	natives/inhabitants of Colmenar

MIMADO ENTRE ALGODONES

Mi sobrino está de un mimado que no hay quien lo aguante. La culpa la tiene su abuela que lo está mimando cada día más. Lo está criando entre algodones. No hay capricho que se le antoje, que no se lo esté dando ya, ¡y así está el niño! Cada vez está más mimado. Tanto es así que no me extraña que en el colegio se estén metiendo siempre con él, que le estén machacando que es un niño mimado.

Tal vez a su abuela no le importe que sea mimoso, que esté todo el tiempo colgado de ella. Pero a mí no. A mí no me gusta que esté pegado a mí el día entero, sin dejarme ni a sol ni a sombra. A mí no me gustan los niños que son pegajosos. Para mí no son simpáticos. Son unos pesados. Cuanto más mimosos son, menos caso les hago yo. Ya pueden estar mimosos conmigo todo lo que quieran, que no me van a sacar ni una gorda. ¡Que se vayan con sus mimos a otra parte!

Vocabulary and Idioms:

Estar mimado:	to be spoilt:
Ser [un niño] mimado:	to be a spoilt child, mollycoddled
Criado entre algodones:	to be pampered, to have a pampered childhood, to be brought up delicately, wrapped in cotton wool; to be born with a silver spoon in one's mouth

Estar mimoso:	to like affectionate attention, to like being mollycoddled, cuddled (HOWN-ESS)
Ser [un niño] mimoso:	to like affectionate attention, to like being mollycoddled, cuddled (WHAT-NESS)
Estar todo el tiempo colgado de alguien:	to be under someone's feet all the time, to hang on someone's apron-strings all day long
Estar pegado a alguien:	lit: to be stuck to someone; fig: to follow someone around constantly; cloying
Ser pegajoso:	to be sticky, cloying; inseperable; to be over-sweet

PEPE EL CHURRETOSO

Pepe está que da pena. Su pelo es un estropajo mugriento, su camisa está más sucia que la de un carbonero, los calcetines con dos buenas papas, y el uniforme está siempre lleno de lamparones, con una manga descosida o con un siete enorme en el culo... Pepe es el chico más sucio y trapajoso de todo el barrio. Si no fuese porque su madre, nada más verle aparecer por la puerta, no lo estuviera metiéndolo ya en el baño, uno creería que Pepe no es que esté negro, sino que es negro: que en verdad su piel es negra. Si no, que lo digan esos carrillos que están siempre manchados de churretes, o esas rodillas con más roña que un guarro, para no tener que hablar de sus manos... Y es que sus manos son dos palas que están siempre llenas de mierda. ¿Cómo va a estar Pepe, pues? Pepe está siempre negro todo él, como el carbón. Más de uno juraría que Pepe es un negrito de pelo rubio.

Pero eso no es lo peor. Pepe es, además, un niño muy sucio y con hábitos asquerosísimos. Siempre se está metiendo el dedo en la nariz, y haciendo cada ruido con la boca que mejor no hablar de ello aquí. Con decir que el niño es asqueroso, ya valga, sin tener que estar entrando en más detalles. ¿Y en educación? Pues en educación está pelado Pepe. En la mesa es un ganso, un auténtico cerdito. En el colegio está siempre castigado, y con razón, por ser tan desobediente. Con sus compañeros es un gallito. Como no lo corrijan a tiempo, va a ser un cerdo de lo más inaguantable el día de mañana. Por desgracia, creo que no puede estar muy bien del coco. Parece que está un poco chiflado. Sus compañeros de clase dicen que está algo tocado del ala, algo ido, y en verdad no están muy equivocados. Por supuesto que esto no justifica que sea un niño tan mal educado. La culpa la tienen sus padres que no lo están corrigiendo. Si yo estuviera encargado de su educación, ya estaría ese niño más derecho que una vela. En lugar de una ducha, le estaría dando yo más palos que a un burro a este Pepe tan guarro y churretoso.

Vocabulary and Idioms:

Estar pelado/a:	lit: to be hairless; fam: to be broke; not to have....
Estar pelado en educación:	to have no manners
Ser un gallito:	fig: to be a show-off
Ser un ganso:	fig: to be sloppy/badly behaved
Ser un cerdito:	to be a little pig
No estar bien del coco:	not to be right in the head
Estar chiflado/a:	to be crazy
Estar algo tocado/a:	to be touched in the head
Estar algo ido/a:	to be crazy, touched
Estar más derecho que una vela:	lit: to be as straight as a candle; fig: to be as straight as a die

UNA TARDE GRIS DE BOSTEZO

Era un día gris.

Un día gris y ordinario, de los muchos días grises y ordinarios con que me castigaba el crudo y tedioso otoño. Todo estaba gris. Monótonamente gris. Pesadamente gris. Como una mancha de aceite espeso, grisáceo, que me ensuciara de gris todo el cuerpo. Hasta mi alma estaba gris aquella tarde de bostezo.

Era un día gris.

Un día más de otoño. Y sin embargo, aquel día estaba más gris que nunca. La tarde estaba gris. El cielo estaba gris... Y para que no quedara nada por estar gris, hasta el aire estaba de un gris ceniza y polvoriento que manchaba de hollín cuanto tocaba: mi huerto, mi casa, mi traje de faena... Era como si la tarde acabara de ser deshollinada, y una nube gris me convirtiera a mí también en ceniza. En polvo de tierra.

Miré a lo alto. El cielo era una masa indistinta de nubes grises, anuciándome aquella tormenta que nunca acababa de llegar. No había llovido todavía aquel otoño. El asfalto de la carretera que siempre había sido de un gris rabioso, estaba con la sequía de un gris decolorido, y su gris ajado se confundía con el gris de la acera de aquella ciudad de cemento. Filas repetidas de pisos y más pisos. Todos iguales. Todos copias que fueran calcadas con el mismo papel gris de calco. Todos desnudos, como habían sido traídos a este mundo por mi mano gris. Sus paredes no estaban pintadas, ni habían sido encaladas, ni aun siquiera revestidas con ningún yeso blanco. Y en medio de tanto gris, estaba en cueros vivos mi casa de cemento. Y el cemento de mi casa estaba hecho ceniza. Y sus tejas que antaño fueran de un gris pizarra, habían perdido ya para siempre sus gris deslumbrante, para pasar a ser gris a secas. Una masa gris. Ceniza. Humo. Polvo.

Era un día gris.

Un día más de mi otoño. De este otoño que iría a ser ya mío para siempre. Y el día estaba gris ceniza, sin otro tono gris que no fuese el gris ceniza de mis ojos.

Miré a mi alrededor. Todo estaba gris, de un gris plomizo monótonamente repetido. La tierra era una sola sombra. Una sombra gris que había sido derramada sobre la tierra. Sobre el aire, la piedra y el agua... Y el gris estaba derramándose generoso sobre mi huerto. Y allí, en mis propias tierras, las cuales eran grises y yermas, yacía mi cuerpo. Como un montón de ceniza más. Como un puñado de tierra. Allí, hecho uno con la tierra. Allí estaba abandonado. Solo. Confundiéndome con el aire, el humo, el agua, el cielo, y la tierra. Allí estaba derramado todo el gris monótono de mi rodar por caminos de polvo, dando vueltas de noria... Todo el gris pesado de mi andar gris ceniza. Gris de plomo.

Allí estaba yo con mi otoño a cuestas. Allí, bajo la pesadez de aquella tarde gris. Pesadamente gris. Monótonamente gris. Inmensamente gris.

Vocabulary and Idioms:

Estar en cueros vivos:	to be stark naked
Ser gris a secas:	to be plain grey
Dar vueltas de noria:	to go round like a waterwheel

CHAPTER EIGHT

A Text Analysis

VIII

Analysis of the use and implication of *ser* and *estar* in the text:

JUAN EL MALAS PULGAS

Juan siempre fue[1] un poco raro pero, desde que le dio por aupar el codo, está[2] como un cencerro. Pena me da de que esté[3] ya tan disparatado y, para colmo de desgracia, [3]más molesto y achacoso que un viejo carcamal. Claro, con eso de que todo se le va en beber y nada en comer, cada día está[4] más chungo. El pobrecillo está[4] pocho con ganas y [4]con más malas pulgas que un chucho callejero... Y así se pasa las horas muertas: hundido en la butaca, en bata, con la boina encajada hasta las cejas, una bufanda reliada al cuello, enroscado como un gato refunfuñón. Allí está[5] Juan, hecho[4] un trapo, ora [4]durmiendo la mona, ora [4]cargando a cuestas con todos sus achaques y dolores. No es que sea[6] muy viejo, que todavía no ha cumplido ni los cincuenta; pero está[6] viejísimo y todo él [6]lleno de arrugas. [7]Como un higo seco. Lo peor no es[8] que esté[9] ya pasado y [9]totalmente calvo (pues Juan es[9] calvo desde que perdió el pelo con la tiña cuando todavía era[9] un buen mozo), ni el que esté[10] tan chupado o [10]chocho (porque en eso da pena ver al triste con lo altivo y gallardo que fue[11] antaño), sino que está[12] de un irritable y quisquilloso que verdaderamente despide a la gente. No es[13] de extrañar, pues, que quien no lo conozca, crea (y con razón) que Juan no es[14] más que un viejo cascarrabias. [14]Un carrañoso. [14]Un abuelito gruñón. Para él, el más mínimo ruido es[15] molesto. El otro día, por ejemplo, fui a hacerle una visita y porque sin querer, al ir a cerrar la puerta, se me fue la mano y dio un portazo, se enfadó como si fuese[16] un niño con rabieta. Y ya estuvo[17] molesto conmigo para el resto de la tarde. Pero eso no es[18] nada. Más molesto se puso el día cuando su ahijado, que es[19] tan imprudente (bueno, el angelito apenas si tiene cinco años), le preguntó que por qué era[20] calvo. Juan le regañó a la pobre criatura, diciéndole que era[21] un mal educado, que hay que ver lo mal educado que estaba[21], que si no le enseñaban educación a los niños de hoy, que bien podría aprender de él a ser[21] educado, y yo qué sé cuántas cosas más... Y para colmo de desgracia (pues iría a provocar una carcajada prematuramente maliciosa en el ahijado), no se le ocurrió otra cosa que chillarle que él no era[22] calvo y que, si estaba[22] calvo, era[23] sólo porque se había afeitado la cabeza, que eso era[24] todo: su cabeza estaba[25] afeitada porque estaba[25] malo. ¡Qué se habría creído el muy indino!, su cabeza no era[26] una bola de billar, ¡vamos con el niño!

1. *Juan siempre **fue** un poco raro*—Juan was always a bit odd: Here the use of *ser (fue)* leaves us in no doubt that *'un poco raro'*, a negative characteristic, is one that has always been identified with Juan and is inherent to his personality—he's always been an odd sort of person.

2. *...pero , desde que le dio por aupar el codo, **está** como un cencerro*—but since he started hitting the booze, he's gone completely off his head:
   Estar is used in the expression *está como un cencerro* firstly because the emphasis here is on Juan's state since (*desde*) he started drinking and does not refer to something that is an inherent characteristic. Further, the word *como (está como)* is another signpost which emphasizes literally 'how' Juan is now behaving, see chapter four, section dealing with states of madness used in expressions employing *estar como*.

3. *Pena me da de que **esté** ya tan disparatado y, para colmo de desgracia, [**esté**] más molesto y [**esté**] achacoso que un viejo carcamal*—I feel really sorry that he's gone completely round the bend, and he's got more complaints and ailments than an

old wreck: Here the use of *estar* with *disparatado* and also (implicitly) with *molesto* and *achacoso* are all very straight-forward cases of howness revealing present states or feelings.

4. *...cada día está más chungo... está pocho con ganas y [está] con más malas pulgas que un chucho callejero...[está] hecho un trapo, ora [está] durmiendo la mona, ora [está] cargando a cuestas con...* As note 3 above, all these expressions inform us of Juan's present state—the way he looks and feels, his appearance, his mood, etc.: ...each day he's more sickly... he looks so rotten and gloomy and is more irritable than a mangy stray... he's good for nothing, he's either sleeping it off, or weighed down by ... In the specific case of *[está] con más malas pulgas...* colloquially the expression *estar con* is synonymous with *tener*, just as *estar con fiebre* = *tener fiebre* (to have a temperature).

5. *Allí está Juan—*
   Estar is used here to indicate Juan's location/position (WHERENESS)

6. *No es que sea muy viejo, que todavía no ha cumplido ni los cincuenta; pero está viejísimo y todo él [está] lleno de arrugas.*
   Ser is employed in the first phrase because this is a specific reference to an essential characteristic of an old man (i.e. old age) and it goes on to say that since Juan does not have this characteristic—as he's not yet fifty—he cannot be defined as such. Thus the intended meaning of the phrase is: *No es que sea [un hombre] muy viejo.*—It's not that he's an old man.
   ...pero está viejísimo y todo él [está] lleno de arrugas.
   In contrast, this phrase refers to Juan's present state—the way he looks: very old and wrinkled.
   See chapter two, section dealing with *viejo/a.*

7. *Como un higo seco* = *[está] como un higo seco.*—He looks like a dried fig.
    See note 2 above.

8. *Lo peor no es que...*—The worst thing is not that...
    See chapter three, section dealing with generalizations and impersonal expressions.

9. *...esté ya pasado y [que esté] totalmente calvo (pues Juan es calvo desde... cuando todavía era un buen mozo)...*
    This sentence is not quite so staightforward as the author is using *ser* and *estar* in a more subtle manner. Here the intended meaning is: the worst thing about Juan is not that his present **state** is one of being past it and completely bald -as Juan lost his hair (became 'a bald man') when he was a handsome youth, due to an illness (ringworm) and thus badlness became an essential, defining or identifying characteristic.
    In the phrase ... *cuando todavía era un buen mozo*—*ser* is again used as this is not a subjective statement about how Juan then appeared, but about 'what' Juan unquestionably then was, i.e. 'a handsome young man' *(un buen mozo)*—and as such he undeniably enjoyed the characteristics of beauty and youth. Besides, the indefinite article *(un/una)* automatically signals identity and requires that *ser* be used.

10. ... *ni el que esté tan chupado o chocho...* This is the straightforward use of *estar* as howness, i.e. looking gaunt and in a doddery state.

11. ... *con lo altivo y gallardo que fue antaño...* Ser is used here as it is an objective observation which identifies Juan (yesteryear—*antaño*) as a proud and gallant [sort of] man.
    See chapter two, section dealing with *alto/a* and *guapo/a*.

12. ... *sino que* **está** *de un irritable y quisquilloso*...
Again this is a straightforward case of 'howness'—his state of being: he is irritable and cantankerous.

13. *No* **es** *de extrañar*...—It's not surprising...
See chapter three, section dealing with impersonal expressions.

14. ...*no* **es** *más que un viejo cascarrabias. [No* **es** *más que]* Un *carrañoso. [No* **es** *más que]* Un *abuelito gruñón.*—... he's just an old grouch. A grumbler. A grumpy old grandpa.
The emphasis here is on 'what' those who do not really know Juan are likely to think of him, i.e. what their concept of Juan would be. As explained in chapter two, when dealing with marital status, and also in note 9 above, the indefinite article *un* clearly indicates definition and hence 'whatness', i.e., he is **un** *[hombre] viejo cascarrabias*...—just **an** old grouch, etc.

15. *Para él, el más mínimo ruido* **es** *molesto.*—For him, the slightest noise is annoying.
This is the case where Juan makes the equation that noise = annoying; and this is 'what' noise (no matter how slight) is for Juan, thus *ser* is used.

16. ... *como si* **fuese** *un niño con rabieta.*—... as if he were a child throwing a tantrum.
This is a straightforward case of 'whatness' and thus *ser* (*fuese*) is used. Further, as in note 14 above, the article *un* indicates definition.

17. *Y ya* **estuvo** *molesto conmigo*...—*And then he was annoyed with me*...
Here *molesto* is used with *estar* and not *ser*, as in note 15 above. This is a clear example of how, in Spanish, the use of the different verbs with the same word (here *molesto*) indicates

whether the intended meaning is that of 'whatness' or 'howness'. In English the all-purpose verb 'to be' does not do this; i.e:

estar molesto — to be annoyed

ser molesto — to be annoying

As we saw earlier, the same is also the case with words like *divertido/a, aburrido/a*, etc...

See chapter four.

18. *Pero eso no es nada.*—But that's nothing.

This is a simple case of whatness: *eso* (that) = *nada* (nothing).

See chapter three, section *Identifying by Equating*.

19. ... *que es [una persona] tan imprudente*—he's so tactless (he's such a tactless person).

Ser is used here as the author indicates that tactlessness is a normal characteristic of a young child.

20. ...*le preguntó que por qué era calvo*—he asked him why he was bald.

The same principle as calvo in note 9 above.

21. ...*que era un mal educado... lo mal educado que estaba... que bien podría aprender de él a ser educado...*

This is another example of where the intended meaning is made clear simply by the use of *ser* and *estar*.

Whatness is plainly intended in the phrases *que era un [niño] mal educado* (that he was an ill-mannered child) and *podría aprender de él a ser [un niño/hombre] educado* (he could learn from him what it is to be a well-mannered child/man). Again the indefinite article is indicating definition.

Whereas the phrase *lo mal educado que estaba* refers to the (bad) way the boy was behaving.

22. *...que él no **era** calvo y que, si **estaba** calvo...*
    In the first phrase—*... que él no **era** calvo*—Juan is saying that he is not really a bald man and he does not want his godson to define him as such.
    Whereas in the second phrase—*y que, si **estaba** calvo [ahora]...* —Juan is here indicating that if he happens to be bald at the present moment, it is not because he is a bald man but merely because he has shaved his head.
    Also see *calvo* in note 9 above.

23. *...**era** sólo porque...*—it was only because...
    See chapter three, section dealing with impersonal expressions.

24. *... que eso **era** todo*—that was all.
    Just as in note 18 above, this is another straightforward case of 'whatness': *eso* (that) = *todo* (all).

25. *... **estaba** afeitada porque **estaba** malo.*— ... it was shaved because he was ill.
    Both phrases here refer to states. For the first case (***estaba** afeitada*) see chapter three, section dealing with *estar* with past participles.

26. *... su cabeza no **era** una bola de billar*—his head was not a billiard ball.
    This is a simple case of 'whatness', defining what his head is not.

Ser and *Estar* Conjugated

CONJUGATION OF *SER*

Infinitive: *ser*
Gerund: *siendo*

Perfect Infinitive: *haber sido*
Perfect Gerund: *habiendo sido*
Past Participle: *sido*

Indicative

Present:

soy
eres
es
somos
sois
son

Perfect:

he   *sido*
has   *sido*
ha   *sido*
hemos   *sido*
habéis   *sido*
han   *sido*

Imperfect:

era
eras
era
éramos
erais
eran

Pluperfect:

había   *sido*
habías   *sido*
había   *sido*
habíamos   *sido*
habíais   *sido*
habían   *sido*

Preterite:

fui
fuiste
fue
fuimos
fuisteis
fueron

Past Anterior*

hube   *sido*
hubiste   *sido*
hubo   *sido*
hubimos   *sido*
hubisteis   *sido*
hubieron   *sido*

* See p. 219

Future:

seré
serás
será
seremos
seréis
serán

Future Perfect:

habré	sido
habrás	sido
habrá	sido
habremos	sido
habréis	sido
habrán	sido

Conditional:

sería
serías
sería
seríamos
seríais
serían

Conditional Perfect:

habría	sido
habrías	sido
habría	sido
habríamos	sido
habríais	sido
habrían	sido

Subjunctive

Present:

sea
seas
sea
seamos
seáis
sean

Perfect:

haya	sido
hayas	sido
haya	sido
hayamos	sido
hayáis	sido
hayan	sido

Imperfect I:

fuera
fueras
fuera
fuéramos
fuerais
fueran

Pluperfect I:

hubiera	sido
hubieras	sido
hubiera	sido
hubiéramos	sido
hubierais	sido
hubieran	sido

Imperfect II:

fuese
fueses
fuese
fuésemos
fueseis
fuesen

Future:*

fuere
fueres
fuere
fuéremos
fuereis
fueren

Pluperfect II:

hubiese   sido
hubieses   sido
hubiese   sido
hubiésemos sido
hubieseis   sido
hubiesen   sido

Future Perfect: *

hubiere   sido
hubieres   sido
hubiere   sido
hubiéremos sido
hubiereis   sido
hubieren   sido

Imperative

Affirmative:

sé (tú)
sea (usted)
seamos
   (nosotros/as)
sed (vosotros/as)

sean (ustedes)

Negative:

no seas (tú)
no sea (usted)
no seamos
   (nosotros/as)
no seáis
   (vosotros/as)
no sean (ustedes)

---

* See p. 219

CONJUGATION OF *ESTAR*

Infinitive: *estar*
Gerund: *estando*

Perfect Infinitive: *haber estado*
Perfect Gerund: *habiendo estado*
Past Participle: *estado*

Indicative

Present:

estoy
estás
está
estamos
estáis
están

Perfect:

he	estado
has	estado
ha	estado
hemos	estado
habéis	estado
han	estado

Imperfect:

estaba
estabas
estaba
estaba
estábamos
estabais
estaban

Pluperfect:

había	estado
habías	estado
había	estado
habíamos	estado
habíais	estado
habían	estado

Preterite:

estuve
etuviste
estuvo
estuvimos
estuvisteis
estuvieron

Past Anterior: *

hube	estado
hubiste	estado
hubo	estado
hubimos	estado
hubisteis	estado
hubieron	estado

---

* see p. 219

Future:

estaré
estarás
estará
estaremos
estaréis
estarán

Future Perfect:

habré   estado
habrás   estado
habrá   estado
habremos   estado
habréis   estado
habrán   estado

Conditional:

estaría
estarías
estaría
estaríamos
estaríais
estarían

Conditional Perfect:

habría   estado
habrías   estado
habría   estado
habríamos   estado
habrías   estado
habríais   estado
habrían   estado

Subjunctive

Present:

esté
estés
esté
estemos
estéis
estén

Perfect:

haya   estado
hayas   estado
haya   estado
hayamos   estado
hayáis   estado
hayan   estado

Imperfect I:

estuviera
estuvieras
estuviera
estuviéramos
estuvierais
estuvieran

Pluperfect I:

hubiera   estado
hubieras   estado
hubiera   estado
hubiéramos estado
hubierais   estado
hubieran   estado

Imperfect II:

estuviese
estuvieses
estuviese
estuviésemos
estuvieseis
estuviesen

Future*:

estuviere
estuvieres
estuviere
estuviéremos
estuviereis
estuvieren

Pluperfect II:

hubiese   estado
hubieses   estado
hubiese   estado
hubiésemos estado
hubieseis estado
hubiesen   estado

Future Perfect*:

hubiere   estado
hubieres   estado
hubiere   estado
hubiéremos estado
hubiereis estado
hubieren   estado

Imperative

Affirmative:

está (tú)
esté (usted)
estemos (nosotros/as)
estad (vosotros/as)
estén (ustedes)

Negative:

no estés (tú)
no esté (usted)
no estemos (nosotros/as)
no estéis (vosotros/as)
no estén (ustedes)

---

* see p. 219

NOTE:

The Past Anterior is rarely used in modern Spanish and then only after temporal clauses depending on conjunctions such as: *cuando* (when), *después que* (after), *luego que* (after), *en cuanto* (as soon as), *tan pronto como* (as soon as), *enseguida que* (as soon as), etc.

The Future Subjunctive is rarely used nowadays, except occasionally in literary language and some colloquial expressions such as *sea lo que fuere* (be that as it may).

The Future Perfect Subjunctive is not used in colloquial Spanish and rarely in literary language. However it is still found in some legal documents.

*   *   *

Spanish Interest Titles from Hippocrene . . .

Spanish-English/ English-Spanish Concise Dictionary (Latin American)
by Ila Warner
500 pages, 4 x 6
0-7818-0261-X
$11.95pb   (0258)

Spanish-English/ English-Spanish Dictionary of Computer Terms
120 pages, 5 ½ x 8 ½
0-7818-0148-6
$16.95   (0036)

Spanish Handy Dictionary
120 pages, 5 x 7 3/4
0-7818-0012-9
$8.95pb   (0189)

Mastering Spanish
by Robert Clark
Book: 338 pages, 5 ½ x 8 ½
0-87052-059-8
$11.95pb   (0527)
2 Cassettes:
0-87052-067-9, $12.95 (0528)

Mastering Advanced Spanish
Book: 326 pages, 5 ½ x 8 ½
0-7818-0081-1, $14.95pb
(0413)
2 Cassettes:
0-7818-0089-7
$12.95pb   (0426)

500 Spanish Words and Phrases
written and edited by Carol Watson & Janet DeSaulles
32 pages, 8 x 10 1/4
color illustrations
0-7818-0262-8
$8.95   (0017)

Spanish-English/ English-Spanish Practical Dictionary
by Arthur S. Butterfield
338 pages, 5 ½ x 8 1/4
0-7818-0179-6
$9.95pb (0211)

All prices subject to change. **TO PURCHASE HIPPOCRENE BOOKS** call (718) 454-2366, or write to: HIPPOCRENE BOOKS, 171 Madison Avenue, New York, NY 10016. Please enclose check or money order, adding $5.00 shipping (UPS) for the first book and $.50 for each additional book.